A high-priority target in warfare is the command-and-control structure of an opponent. That is why the American family and the moral values that fortify it are under relentless assault. Josiah O'Neil understands this critical truth and dares to say it. Josiah is unafraid to stare evil in the face and call it what it is–EVIL. *Defining Truth* will help others have the courage to stand up and speak up.

Tony Perkins, President
Family Research Council & Host of Washington Watch

DEFINING TRUTH

ARTICULATING AMERICA'S WORLD VIEW

JOSIAH O'NEIL

FOREWORD BY PASTOR JACK HIBBS

book**Villages**

To my beautiful wife, Lindsay, whose tenacity for God's Word and dedication to truth has kept me in line over the years. And, to America–may her sons and daughters remember God's providential hand in their nation and return to His loving arms before it is too late.

Contents

Foreword

Beyond any shadow of a doubt, information is the most valuable piece of the puzzle board in the world in which we live. Throughout human history, whoever held the most accurate and detailed information had the upper hand, whether that be for the building of the ancient monoliths or in the stratagems needed to oppose an enemy by knowing their next move before it was made–truth is essential to victory.

Josiah O'Neil is a man who has served many years in the area of security operations and their execution to defend and protect not only the United States of America, but other countries as well. He has been a crucial part of the United States Army and protective detail operations in both private sector security and government entities such as the United States Diplomatic Security Service, which qualified him to provide protection for our nation's top individuals and allies in some of the most hostile and dangerous regions on earth. Josiah also spent ten years in law enforcement, both as a police officer and deputy sheriff, and later as a Special Agent with the U.S. State Department serving under then Secretary of State Michael Pompeo.

In addition to the security, military, and law enforcement experience, Josiah spent many years on the mission field under his parents who were missionaries with Calvary Chapel for over thirty years in Latin America. Having gone through most of his schooling in Mexico, he completed his high school years in a bilingual collegiate in Cuenca, Ecuador. This firm background in the expositional teaching of God's Word gives Josiah the foundation from which to launch his apologetic perspective on culture from a Christian-Judaic worldview. His experience, knowledge, and skill have equipped him to write this book and provide you with vital information for your family's understanding of truth and

9

that of our nation amidst the clamor of nonsense in today's age of information and rhetoric.

During the colonial period, Sir Edmund Burke stated to the British Parliament, "The only thing necessary for the triumph of evil is for good men to do nothing." Josiah understands the critical elements needed to defend a culture for good. His passion is to equip and mobilize all those who love truth and what is good. I have known Josiah for decades; he is a man who has been consistent, steadfast, and faithful to the mission, to his family, and to God.

I encourage you to read this book, hoping you will take away tangible, practical knowledge and information that will allow you to utilize it in your day-to-day life. I pray that it will challenge your way of thinking in these days of uncertainty. Its instruction and information could very well save your life. May you find this a tremendous tool in preserving freedom both personally and publicly as we fight to defend our families, our culture, and our nation.

Jack Hibbs
Senior Pastor, Calvary Chapel Chino Hills

Acknowledgements

I would be remiss not to immediately state the obvious, that without the providential hand of God I would not have life, much less anything to write a book about. It was God's written word that daily renewed my resolve to put forth an apologetic stance for what He has so aptly wrought by His own hand in America.

I would like to thank my family, specifically my wife, Lindsay, and our three children–Scarlett, Emma, and Connor–who have tolerated many late nights without their dad as I toiled over research and editing.

I would like to thank Pastor Jack Hibbs, whose dedication to support this effort and whose own faithfulness in the ministry has inspired countless individuals to rise and take a stand. I am thankful for Tony Perkins, whose leadership at the Family Research Council has ensured a national voice for Christians in Washington, DC, and influenced countless policy decisions by their tireless, often thankless work. I am grateful for the authors of the many works I used during my research, one of which was William Federer, who took the time to answer phone calls when I needed a historical answer, despite being very busy himself. And I am thankful for the unnamed pastors all over this country who, bring the truth of God to His people through expositional teaching, the lack of which would mean the certain demise of this nation.

And lastly to my parents, Kevin and Diane O'Neil, whose years of service on the mission field and steadfast dedication to ingrain in me a love of Christ and a sense of gratitude for the nation of our birth made me who I am. Pop, I know you'd be proud of this book. I'll see you soon.

Chapter 1

Truth

What is truth?

Is truth subjective? Is truth defined by whoever declares it to be true? Is truth relative to modern standards? Is it, like proverbial beauty, found in the eye of the beholder? Is it, as an Eastern philosopher might posit, created by the observer?

I submit to you that truth is absolute and unhindered by one's opinion of it, and that the evidence for this assertion is reality itself.

I recently watched an interview where a young person was asked by the interviewer if they believed that reality was subjective. The young person said that it was, stating that reality was whatever a person wanted it to be. The interviewer then asked, "So if I say you don't exist, do you not exist?"

The young person responded, "If you say I don't exist, then I don't exist." As unbelievably stupid as that response may seem, an untold number of people in today's world currently hold this same perspective.

We could embark on a discussion of the Left's ideological origins, of Marxism and its effect upon Western philosophy, or of secular humanism, but in an effort to keep things short, let's stick with defining truth from a realist's perspective.

Cause and Effect

If you punch a wall (unless you have a degenerative nerve disease or something precluding you from feeling), you will most certainly feel the effect of such an action immediately. This is an undeniable reality. The wall, much like your nervous system, does not care about an observer's perspective or how they feel about you punching the wall. It simply complies with physics and responds accordingly.

In a similar way, actions taken by people are subject to cause and effect. As Sir Isaac Newton clarified, for every action there is an equal and opposite reaction. Philosophically speaking, one can see this plainly in the world around us as experienced through every variety of relationship. The way we treat our friends, family, and loved ones has an obvious effect on our daily lives. Likewise, the way we treat strangers often dictates their reaction toward us. On a grander scale, decisions made by governments (at all levels) also have very real effects, whether positive in the form of growth or negative in the form of consequence. Despite one's philosophical stance, the undeniable truth is that reality dictates what truth is; this is not negotiable.

Detractors would argue that if you remove choice from the equation, then there can be no right or wrong because it is not in the individual's control. Let me clarify. If I choose to do something, then one can rightly argue that I am at fault for the consequences of my choices, whatever they may be. But if I argue that no choice was involved–that I was a product of my environment or circumstances–then it would be unjust to assign responsibility for whatever occurred.

Herein lies the crux of leftists' efforts to remove all traces of Christian-Judaic values from Western civilization, as it is those values that assign personal responsibility and autonomy to individuals. The secular humanist believes that all humans are merely highly evolved animals, coming from nowhere, with no final destination. In contrast, the Christian-Judaic perspective, and by and large all of Western civilization, would argue that human beings are created with purpose and will someday give an answer for what they've done or not done. This unquestionably means humans are responsible for what they do. They are, in a word, accountable.

Accountability dictates whether an action is good or bad because reality demands a standard from which no person is exempt. The fact that all people eventually die is nonnegotiable; this is an inescapable truth that festers in the relativist's mind. If death is inevitable, what else is absolute? If someone tells you there is no absolute truth, you should ask them if that is true or not.

Every action demands a reaction from which no person is excused. As a result, we can interpret the inherent goodness of said action by its results. The Bible makes this painfully evident in Romans 6:23, where it says, "The wages of sin is death, but the gift of God is eternal life in Christ Jesus our Lord" (NKJV). What the apostle Paul was explaining to the Romans in that verse is simply that the natural and scientific law of cause and effect was redeemed by the very Creator of those laws.

It's not that the law itself was abolished, but rather the Author of the law took the consequence of wrongdoing upon Himself, thereby releasing the blameworthy of their accountability. This concept is deeply ingrained into Christian-Judaic beliefs, and therefore it is deeply entwined in America's cultural roots. The effects of incorporating personal responsibility and accountability into American government and society have been astronomical compared to previous government models and have led to the greatest, most benevolent nation the world has ever seen.

Overcoming Self

Having established that reality is inescapable and that Newton's third law demands recognition of cause and effect, all that remains is to determine whether or not the causes of those inescapable reactions are good or bad.

I suggest the measure for doing so is to determine whether the "effect" in cause and effect is negative or positive. If the effect is negative, then the cause is wrong, despite the length of time required to prove so. This would not be that difficult except for one great obstacle: the self. The self would resist this simple test out of sheer passion for pleasure. This is why the addict cannot stop using dangerous drugs despite the horrible effects they have on their life.

The drive to obtain pleasure is so strong, it causes individuals to deny the reality of consequences that are so painfully obvious and detrimental. This concept applies equally to psychological pursuits. The self prevents us from seeing reality, which in turn prevents us from acknowledging absolute truth. Truth is not so much relative as it is difficult to submit to. In that context, the intellectual and Christian apologist G. K. Chesterton, in his book *What's Wrong with the World*, wrote, "The Christian ideal has not been tried and found wanting. It has been found difficult; and left untried."[1]

Self-worship is the ultimate betrayal of reality and of those around us. It inherently ignores the hurtful effects of self-gratification on others, choosing rather to seek pleasure at all expense. The secular humanist's worldview, having refused the existence of a higher power, deifies self-interest, while in contrast the Christian-Judaic worldview, and by and large all of Western civilization, holds self-denial as the ultimate intrinsic aim in life.

"What does this have to do with defining truth?" you may ask. Self-exultation is the largest detriment to accepting reality because if one's worldview is premised on ignoring the natural world and its plainly observable laws, then one has only oneself to satisfy in the end. The end goal of all action, therefore, becomes pleasure at the expense of all else. A corrupt perspective on reality produces this inward navel-gazing, which by definition does not succeed because it is not founded in reality.

Turning to self and to one's emotions is highly misleading, and ultimately ends in confusion and consequence. As Jeremiah 17:9 so clearly delineates, "The heart is deceitful above all things, and desperately sick; who can understand it?" The negative impact of the pursuit of pleasure is plainly seen in the world around us. When people turn inward and can see nothing but the elevation of self, everything around them is eventually destroyed. Proverbs 25:28 says, "A man without self-control is like a city broken into and left without walls."

In describing the struggle of obsessive inward gazing in a letter to Edward Lofstrom, C. S. Lewis wrote, "You are of course perfectly right in defining your problem (which is also mine and everyone's) as 'excessive selfness.'" He went on to say, "All have this disease: fortunate are the minority who know they have it."[2] Lewis completed this thought to a friend by referring to the biblical book of 1 John, which says, "By this we shall know that we are of the truth and reassure our heart before him; for whenever our heart condemns us, God is greater than our heart, and he knows everything" (3:19-20). Western civilization (and thereby conservatism) is premised on the Christian-Judaic worldview, which in turn is founded on the concept of created beings whose truth is dependent upon a Definer of truth.

Perhaps the most dangerous aspect of self-worship that defines our culture today is the fact that truths are determined through the lens of emotions, which have replaced the Definer of truth. In other words, truth is relative to how one feels about it. This is very dangerous, as one person's "felt reality" may differ greatly from another's, and in some cases may cause physical harm. Say, for example, one person's "truth" is that everything their neighbor owns should belong to them. In our self-worshipping culture, who is to tell them otherwise? Is not reality relative to the observer? So what happens when your neighbor believes everything you own belongs to him? Whose reality wins? This may seem far-fetched, but it is in fact playing out before us around the world as secular humanists vie for control and power.

Klaus Schwab, leader of the World Economic Forum, recently stated, "You'll own nothing, and you'll be happy" (The Great Reset, 2020). The dominant power will define their own reality for a time, and then all must comply or be removed. This has played out in history time and time again. Historical propaganda shows that repeatedly telling a lie will lead to people accepting the lie as truth. This can be extremely dangerous, such as when the Nazis convinced an entire population that Jews were evil and deserving of eradication, or when the Soviet Union allowed millions of people to starve to death in Ukraine rather than allow dissent against the leftist government. Ultimately what history has shown us is that behavior contrary to reality and its consequences is short-lived, and almost always leads to great human suffering.

The Christian-Judaic worldview holds that the pleasures of sin are "fleeting" (Hebrews 11:25), and I propose this is mainly because the offender, lost in the pursuit of pleasure, is unaware of or unconcerned with the negative impact their actions have on society around them.

The terminal pursuit of self is exemplified in a person willing to hurt anyone and everyone who prevents their pursuit of self-gratification–the ultimate indifference to reality. People chase paramount self-gratification by deceiving themselves about the effects of their own actions instead of acknowledging the damage their selfishness causes to those around them. This is pervasive in modern culture because of a leftist ideological movement that has convinced the population that truth does not exist outside of one's relative definition.

Bad Foundation

Let me give you a practical example. Imagine a person says, "I believe in flying unicorns," because they decided they wanted to believe that unicorns existed. The thought of flying unicorns makes them feel good, and they like the idea of it, despite the reality that they don't exist. Then, based on this belief, this unicorn dreamer sets out to construct a building, telling the construction workers that flying unicorns will lift the heavy objects up to the top of the building as the project rises into the sky. No matter how intelligent this self-deceived person may be, no matter how much money they have, no matter how many individuals they convince to assist them in this effort, they will not succeed–because flying unicorns do not exist.

So, too, is the leftist who denies the reality of the world around them and attempts to build a society based on the faulty premise of relativism. But as the television show *Reading Rainbow* would say, "Don't take my word for it." The advantage of being a realist, besides the fact that reality and facts are most often on your side, is the ability to learn from history, which tells of the great failures of man. One can look at history and see for oneself what has failed and what has succeeded. In the case of the leftist, history is not their friend. The failures of secular humanists and their efforts to usurp God in society have led to the greatest human tragedies man has ever known. More people died in the twentieth century alone than in the previous nineteen centuries combined as a direct result of secular governments playing God with their cultures. (generally attributed to Eric Hobsbawm in his book, *The Age of Extremes: The Short Twentieth Century, 1914-1991.*)

Communists, socialists, Marxists, Nazis, Maoists, and many more embraced man as the center of humanity's purpose, denying the existence of a Creator and worshipping self in God's place. A casual perusal of these governments throughout history will show that many millions of people died as a result of denying reality and, in essence, refusing to acknowledge absolute truth. The Holocaust, the starvation of Soviets, the mass murder of dissidents, the oppression of dissenting opinions are all a product of man's attempt to replace the reality of cause and effect. These deaths should not be taken lightly. Western civilization has been exceptional, not in the fact that human beings didn't make mistakes but rather in the belief that mistakes are to be dealt with and learned from, because we believe that humans are in fact accountable for their actions.

This is what America's founding members understood and deeply respected when shaping the nation's founding documents. They concluded that while the government should make no laws prohibiting the free practice of any religion, adherence to

Christian-Judaic values was essential for success. All individuals benefit from a society that begins with the premise that truth must be defined by reality. It is this foundation of truth upon which all else is built. Any other approach will fail, and history has shown this to be fact. You don't have to be a religious person to see that everyone benefits from a Christian-Judaic worldview in Western civilization. It was this worldview that freed Europe from Nazis. It was this belief that held back the tide of communism from destroying millions of lives around the world. It was this belief that ended slavery in America. It is this belief that allows for individuals to flourish under capitalist systems that enable the United States to be the most benevolent nation to have ever existed. This Christian-Judaic form of government stands as the last bastion of peace in the world today, and it must be ardently defended.

Western Civilization's Acknowledgment of Truth

Acknowledging truth as intrinsic, absolute, and externally derived (that is, from outside oneself) was crucial in forming Western civilization's worldview. We see this truth constantly gnawing at the consciences of the early Americans as the practice of slavery persisted despite the founders' desire to have it done away with. The secular humanist would argue that truths, being relative to each man, must be weighed against the popular opinion for veracity. Therefore if the mob says it is good, then it must be good. This leads to very real problems once an individual is confronted with the reality (the premise of truth they so adamantly deny) that not all in a society agree with them all the time.

   Just as mob rule can be deceptive and disguise the truth of a situation, so the evil of slavery was obscured by man's ambition and avarice. While secular humanists had a difficult time convincing the mob of the evil inherent to the institution of slavery, it was only those who clung to an external source of wisdom that relied on an unchanging definition of truth to guide their effort: Christians.

   It was well known that the founders opposed slavery and

believed that it was not viable with the goal of creating a free nation founded on biblical principles. But religion had become amalgamated with the ambition of men, twisted to serve their own purposes. Many times in history, mankind has used Christian belief in word only, failing to practice what Jesus taught and falsely portraying themselves as righteous. The Bible condemns false teachers and religious people who use the pretense of righteousness for wrongdoing.

On misleading those in the Church or causing others to fail, the Bible says in Luke 17:2, "It would be better for him if a millstone were hung around his neck and he were cast into the sea than that he should cause one of these little ones to sin." Also, in Hebrews 13:17, speaking on why we should submit to authority, the Bible includes the stipulation that leaders are accountable for what they lead people to believe, "for they are keeping watch over your souls, as those who will have to give an account." While someone who is uneducated in Christian ideology may be easily confused by these pretentious leaders who pop up throughout history, true adherents to the Scriptures can see right through their lies and, so understanding the truth, are able to give a defense of what is right. Only by adherence to the truth itself can one accurately and rightly divide truth from wrong; this is discernment.

The Christian-Judaic worldview holds that knowledge and truth come from the Creator and therefore by studying and applying the Word of God in our daily lives. James 1:5 says, "If any of you lacks wisdom, let him ask God, who gives generously to all without reproach, and it will be given him." But that promise does not come without an obligation. If you keep reading, in verses 6 and 8 James continued, "But let him ask in faith, with no doubting, for the one who doubts is like a wave of the sea that is driven and tossed by the wind. . . . He is a double-minded man, unstable in all his ways." Again we see the Christian-Judaic perspective concerning those who claim to apply truth to ideologies they espouse yet do so inaccurately with hidden motivations; these are accountable and guilty of wrong.

We see this very powerfully exemplified in the tumultuous events leading up to the American Civil War regarding slavery and whether or not it was supported by Christian values. While the founders had made it abundantly clear that slavery was something that should and would eventually disappear in American culture, slavery persisted way beyond their expectations and became the center of great conflict between Southern states, whose economy depended on slave labor, and the Northern states, who increasingly supported the abolitionist movement, mainly led by Christian Republicans.

To this point, the elected vice president of the Confederate States of America, Alexander Stephens, wrote this concerning slavery and the Confederate Constitution in 1861:

[Thomas] Jefferson, in his forecast, had anticipated this, as the "rock upon which the old Union would split." He was right. What was conjecture with him, is now a realized fact. But whether he fully comprehended the great truth upon which that rock stood and stands, may be doubted. The prevailing ideas entertained by him and most of the leading statesmen at the time of the formation of the old constitution, were that the enslavement of the African was in violation of the laws of nature; that it was wrong in principle, socially, morally, and politically. It was an evil they knew not well how to deal with, but the general opinion of the men of that day was that, somehow or other in the order of Providence, the institution would be evanescent and pass away. This idea, though not incorporated in the constitution, was the prevailing idea at that time.[3]

So this is what the Confederates and proslavery promoters thought about the founding fathers? In Stephens's own words, the founders believed that slavery was "wrong in principle, socially, morally, and politically . . . an evil they knew not well how to deal with." One famous founder, Patrick Henry, fueled by a Christian-

Judaic worldview said, "Slavery is detested; we feel its fatal effects; we deplore it with all the pity of humanity."[4] When slavery eventually fell, it was undoubtedly the fuel of Christian perspective that drove men to accountability. America didn't start slavery, but it certainly ended it, by men who believed in absolute truth.

In John 15:25-27, Jesus said, "'They hated me without a cause.' But when the Helper comes, whom I will send to you from the Father, the Spirit of truth, who proceeds from the Father, he will bear witness about me. And you also will bear witness, because you have been with me from the beginning.'"

We will cease to exist if we turn our backs on everything we know to be real and exchange truth for a self-seeking, ideological fantasy. Truth can only be defined by reality, and we must preserve this societal concept. Romans 1:18 says that men "by their unrighteousness suppress the truth" because what can be known of God is obvious even in the natural world around them. Verse 25 goes on to say, "They exchanged the truth about God for a lie and worshiped and served the creature rather than the Creator." Lies have always been at the center of suffering. Wherever lies prevail, failure follows. Wherever truth is acknowledged, life abounds. Truth is inextricably tied to reality, and anyone in culture who seeks to undermine basic reality should be adamantly opposed.

Chapter 2
Love

What is love?

According to secular combatants in the culture war, love is nothing more than acquiescence, the surrendering to one's ultimate desire regardless of its alignment with reality. The secular humanist is readily prepared to accept anything, and without protest, regardless of how negative the outcome may be. This perspective, however emotionally provocative it may seem at first glance, leads to nothing but suffering.

When you were a child, did your parents ever tell you to do something you didn't want to do? Perhaps frustrated by the denial, a child in such circumstances will throw a temper tantrum or sulk away into a back bedroom to show outward disdain for their caretaker's choice–but in reality, who knows best? If your parent told you not to touch the hot stove, was it because they hated you? Or is it not more accurate to say it was because they loved you and did not want you to be hurt that they stopped you from acting? These commonsense examples may seem infantile, but in fact they present deep truths in today's culture war.

The World's Lie

The secular humanist determines love to be unobstructed desire, and anyone who dares to prevent one's personal desire is labeled a bigot, and therefore opposed to love. Yet reality (specifically in light of cause and effect) proves this to be false. Does unfettered emotional fulfillment truly define love? No, it does not. Let us consider some practical examples through the lens of reality.

Imagine for a moment a family member or close friend who suffers with drug addiction. This addiction has caused major upheaval in their lives and has hurt those closest to them. The drug addiction is both mentally and physically deleterious and leads to a litany of subsidiary problems that cause both the individual and those around them to suffer. Furthermore, the individual's desire to fulfill their lusts for pleasure also damages society, as their drug addiction leads to thefts, arrests, and burdens upon taxpayers. Now consider the secular humanist's definition of love, whereby one is not allowed to challenge the individual's pursuit of pleasure. Can it really be said that love is allowing a person to do whatever they want regardless of the consequence?

Which of these two perspectives would we consider loving: telling the addict the truth and risking being labeled a bigot, or enabling them to continue abusing dangerous drugs and self-righteously declaring our love for all?

Now let us deal with the drug addict from a sagacious perspective as observed by the verity of the damage the individual has caused both themselves and society. If you truly care for the addict, will you not tell them the truth concerning the effects of their actions? Will you not attempt to reconcile this individual with reality? True love would require you to do so. Love would demand you tell this person the truth, that their actions are hurting both themselves and the people around them. Love would seek help; love would desire recovery; love would present options for change; love would never enable the isolated damaging of its recipient; love would never be defined as only condoning and encouraging pleasure at all costs. This is reality.

So, too, with all human suffering: love demands accordance with reality. In whatever circumstance it can be applied, love is required to conform to the reality of either the damage or the benefit it contributes to. Whether that reality deals primarily with geopolitical issues, political issues, or those of a personal nature, it must by definition benefit the recipient in the long run. I note "long run" because it is commonly understood that the pursuit of self can be pleasurable for a time. But it is equally understood that all selfish pursuits come to an end and most often cause suffering to those around us along the way.

Love According to the Christian-Judaic Worldview

Let us contrast the secular humanist's definition of love with that of the Christian-Judaic or Western worldview, which conspicuously marked the foundations of the American republic. In comparison to the secular definition of love, which is defined by support of one's emotional impulse, the Christian defines love as actions framed by self-denial in pursuit of another's gain, ultimately exemplified by Christ's sacrifice on the cross. The greatness of love defined in this manner is that it always entails self-sacrifice as opposed to self-exultation. Philippians 2:3 says, "Do nothing from selfish ambition or conceit, but in humility count others more significant than yourselves."

For the Christian, if an assertion of love does not conform to reality–in this context, to the benefit of the recipient–it is not love by definition. The Christian-Judaic worldview requires the adherent to submit their action to the test of realistic applicability. We see this perspective encouraged in Acts 17:11, where the apostle Paul said, "They received the word with all eagerness, examining the Scriptures daily to see if these things were [true]." It is apparent that God desires individuals to diligently study Scripture to determine the veracity of what it says. That is, the Bible requires its followers to test whether or not its words ring true, as compared to reality. The validity of love is continually compared to truth, specifically in contrast to selfish ambition.

In Philippians 1:15-18, Paul wrote that some Christians were teaching others about Jesus out of "envy and rivalry" while others were doing so out of "good will." The two motivations were then characterized as being "selfish ambition" or "love." Paul then dove deeper and described the motivations as being grounded in "truth" (love) or "pretense" (selfish ambition). So the Christian must define love as an action that is grounded in reality and truth and is not self-seeking or pretentious. When someone is acting in a way that is harmful to themselves or others, love will present truth that is good for the recipient in the long run. By contrast, the selfish person will present flattery (pretense), most often in a self-gratifying attempt to remove themselves from hardship. This ultimately damages the recipient because it is not grounded in reality.

I once stood over a deceased man who had overdosed on fentanyl. As the paramedics prepared to move the corpse into the transport van, a man arrived on the scene and identified himself as the deceased man's brother. Saddened by the news, the brother told police he had just seen his brother alive the day before, at that same location, homeless on the street. This man told the police he had brought his brother a clean needle for him to use to inject his drugs. Unfortunately, that was the very same needle his brother had used to administer his fatal dose of narcotics. The needle was the last thing the man ever gave his brother, and he used it to kill himself. I recall the man being distraught by his action and repeatedly stating how stupid he was for doing so as his brother's body was loaded into the coroner's vehicle.

Enabling wrongdoing and avoiding reality in circumstances is never a wise choice. Those who continually alter reality when truth is so painfully obvious should be examined carefully for ulterior, selfish, or undisclosed motives. Proverbs 27:5-6 says, "Better is open rebuke than hidden love. Faithful are the wounds of a friend; profuse are the kisses of an enemy."

Chapter 3

Purpose

What is the purpose of life?

What is the purpose of a goal, either short term or long term? What motivates purpose in general? Is there a difference in perspective on what the purpose of life is between the left and right spectrums of ideological movements in the world today?

In the following paragraphs we will explore this as well as what those differences are and why they are so different. In essence, the Left is confined by an evolutionary perspective that limits their purpose to the tangible that they are living right now and nothing more; this inevitably leads to an ends-justifies-the-means outcome as the pursuit of self dominates all else. The Right's perspective, in contrast, is boundless, framed by the metaphysical rather than limited by the finite life spans of mankind and sworn to fulfill innate desires placed in all humans by their Creator.

What Is Purpose Without a Purpose-Giver?

In his 1882 "Parable of the Madman," Friedrich Nietzsche famously described a madman shouting to wary onlookers in the marketplace that God was dead: "The madman jumped into their midst and pierced them with his eyes. 'Whither is God?' he cried; 'I will tell you. *We have killed him*–you and I. All of us are his murderers.'"[1] Nietzsche was simply describing parabolically the cultural shift he foresaw as secularism invaded Western civilization that was once loyal to Christian-Judaic perspectives. What perhaps is more interesting than a secularist declaring their killing of a sovereign (ideologically) is Nietzsche's questioning of the void, which now must be filled because of the lack of purpose and moral clarification. To this point he said,

> How shall we comfort ourselves, the murderers of all murderers? What was holiest and mightiest of all that the world has yet owned has bled to death under our knives: who will wipe this blood off us? What water is there for us to clean ourselves? What festivals of atonement, what sacred games shall we have to invent? Is not the greatness of this deed too great for us? Must we ourselves not become gods simply to appear worthy of it?[2]

Secularists, as Nietzsche so poignantly described, are forced to fill the inevitable vacuum that is formed when created beings deny their Creator and seek to internalize the power that motivates purpose. This vacuum not only represents a lack of moral authority but also a lack of purpose, destination, and philosophical direction for society. We see this clearly in the violence and death brought on by secularist governments of the twentieth century. Could the Nazi regime have convinced their notoriously evil death squadrons to burn Jews in ovens by the millions had they not first declared that God was dead? Richard Weikart, in his book *From Darwin to Hitler*, said, "No matter how crooked the road was from Darwin to Hitler, clearly Darwinism and eugenics smoothed the path for Nazi ideology, especially for the Nazi stress on expansion, war, racial struggle, and racial extermination."[3]

But, one might ask, what does this have to do with Nietzsche's "Parable of the Madman"? The simple answer is this: when replacing reality with man's own invention of causation and purpose, you are left with a false representation of reality instead of the real thing. This leads to chaos, a purposeless existence. The more astute among those who have wholeheartedly rejected the notion of a Creator are quick to admit the futility of life, thus adopting a nihilist worldview–from dust to dust and nothing after. But as astute as the fatalists may be, they are consistently bereft in providing clear explanations for the intangible aspects of human nature, such as the soul, emotion, and the self-awareness of mankind.

But Nietzsche, and others like him, was not incipient in suggesting that God was dead societally speaking. Thousands of years before, the Bible not only identified the purpose of life as being inextricably tied to the Creator but foresaw man's desire to suggest otherwise. Romans 1:25 tells us that "they exchanged the truth about God for a lie and worshiped and served the creature rather than the Creator." Yet even this mention of man's usurpation in the book of Romans is not the first time we observe the seed of confusion and chaos. It appears for the first time in the aptly named story of the Fall in the book of Genesis.

Satan, appearing in the form of a serpent, convinces Eve that God has deceived her and that the Creator only forbade her from eating the fruit of the forbidden tree because He knew if she did so, she would become like Him. In essence, by disobeying God's order she would become like God Himself, making the Creator irrelevant. Genesis 3:5 chronicles the serpent speaking to Eve, saying, "For God knows that when you eat of it your eyes will be opened, and *you will be like God*" (emphasis added). So it seems Nietzsche was not the first to posit that God was dead and man would replace Him. In both the case of the Genesis story and Nietzsche's madman parable, this idea was not true, and as secular governments throughout history soon proved, denying reality comes at a great cost.

Thus a pattern emerges, perceived by Christians through a lens of truth, which reveals the same spirit instigating most of history's evil. The same spirit that convinced Eve that God was denying her some unseen reality, a chance to be a deity, is the same spirit that motivated Nietzsche to author his fatalistic parable of the death of God. It is also the same spirit that drove Hitler as he viewed the world through a secular humanist spyglass, seeing nothing but animalistic ventures by animalistic beings. This same spirit drove Darwin to explain his racist theory of evolution and sparked revolution among Bolsheviks vying for power in a godless Russia. In essence, it is a world stage upon which there are two opposing forces: good and evil, God and Satan, purporse or futility.

In contrast to the Christian-Judaic perspective, the sense of purpose for the secular humanist is constantly shifting based on whatever self-pleasing goal may present itself. Purpose varies throughout history; without constant truth by which to define itself, it struggles in the quandary of relativity and constant reinvention. Purpose is tossed to and fro in the sea of humanism as wave after wave of baseless ideology, intent on distracting the adherent from truth, confuses and blinds the drowning swimmer.

Because the Christian recognizes reality–that existence stems from a Creator–it follows that the purpose of all existence is then guided by the One who created it, on an unchanging path extending through the ages, never altered, never fading. Purpose is derived from uncompromising truth. There is a moral law because of a moral Law-Giver, a purpose because of a Purpose-Giver.

Purpose Driven by Accountability

And so the Christian and the Christian-Judaic worldview hold that because there is a Purpose-Giver, there is therefore a philosophical litmus by which action must be tested, culminating not in death but in the life that follows. Western civilization's understanding of purpose can be summarized in one word: accountability.

Accountability's greatest antagonist is pride: the desire to please self above all, the refusal to submit, the ultimate self-exultation, the precedent to failure. The person who first submits to the reality that we are not self-generated, that we are created and purposefully made, thereby accepts that they are accountable to an Authority outside of themselves. This is a moral Law-Giver who, being above the plane of human existence, judges the actions of man by a higher standard than man himself can generate. Furthermore, the Christian-Judaic worldview holds that these moral laws are self-evident and innate in all human beings, who being born of a Creator are endowed with inalienable truths understood even without being taught. As Romans 1:20 says of mankind's knowledge of a Creator, "His invisible attributes, namely, his eternal power and divine nature, have been clearly perceived, ever since the creation of the world, in the things that have been made. So they are without excuse."

Guided by these truths, Western civilization understood that the actions of man were to be judged and therefore were conducted with purpose leading to alignment with the Creator's will. To clarify, the general will of God is that all mankind understand reality and know the Creator. The gospel, God's message of salvation to all mankind, is illuminated in 1 Timothy 2:4-6, which says that God "desires all people to be saved and to come to the knowledge of the truth. For there is one God, and there is one mediator between God and men, the man Christ Jesus, who gave himself as a ransom for all." Because the laws of cause and effect are as true in the metaphysical realm as they are in the physical, we are indebted to a Creator whose standard is unattainable. Mankind is deficient in capacity to achieve God-like perfection. In the very antithesis of what Satan proposed to Eve in the garden, God Himself becomes the propitiation for our lacking and allows us access to what otherwise is unreachable. Here is where purpose is born: God, who created mankind, being outside the confines of time itself, has foreseen all actions to be taken by man and determined us to be wanting. He therefore replaces our weakness with victory through His sacrifice, and upon our realization of this reality and acceptance of His gift, He provides for us in Himself a purpose for living and a guide by which to do so.

On this foundation Western civilization adapts the biblical perspective for all actions, those in our most intimate of relationships as well as those in society and government alike.

The Bible becomes then a guidebook or a map, as it were, for life itself and how we are to conduct ourselves toward our fellow man and the Creator. The Christian theologian would delve deeper into God's general will and God's specific will, learned by studying the Creator's revealed word, but it is sufficient to say for the adherent to the Christian-Judaic worldview there is now a clearly defined purpose for everything. This purpose gives Western civilization a clear answer to what is right or wrong, true or false–a guide to how we are to conduct ourselves throughout life. The very knowledge of this truth provides the adherent accountability, for it is knowledge of the law that allows one to be held accountable for one's actions. The truth of God is as a posted sign. When there is no understanding, the sign can have no hold over the observer, for in their ignorance they do not understand. But once the posted law is understood, the reader is fully aware there no longer exists an excuse for disobeying it. The sign is there for a reason, always for the reader's benefit, out of love, and with purpose. The laws of the universe exist to point man toward his Creator.

The Natural and Conceptual Laws Collide

The founders of the American republic inevitably saw the connection between the Purpose-Giver and His care for creation exemplified in Ecclesiastes 3. Solomon expounded on the fragility of man and God's eternal perspective. Specifically, he claimed that God is just because man, whom God created, is made with purpose and possesses innate knowledge of the Creator. Therefore, having knowledge of the truth is without excuse. Verse 17 says, "God shall judge the righteous and the wicked, for there is a time there for every purpose and for every work" (NKJV). Purpose is built into creation itself, and the reality of life is undeniably evident in the natural world, just as it is in the undulating world of secular humanists attempting to explain the meaning of life.

One incredible example of purpose built into the known universe can be seen in the relationship between conceptual mathematics and physical laws. While mathematical law is conceptual and exists only in the mind, the universe abides by these mathematical laws. In his book *Fractals: The Secret Code of Creation*, author Jason Lisle expounded on the incredible Mandelbrot set, a mathematical equation in a branch of mathematics known as complex dynamics.

"This field involves sets of numbers," Lisle wrote, "that are defined by functions that involve iteration–that is, doing a calculation repeatedly."[4] The Mandelbrot set exemplifies clear and mathematical laws showing reliable repetition and guidelines, purposeful design, and purpose. When applied to a computer algorithm and imagery, the Mandelbrot set reveals beautiful images and complex designs unfathomable to the human mind. According to one online article, "It is great fun to calculate elements of the Mandelbrot set and to plot them. The resulting set is endlessly complicated." Regarding its complexity and difficulty to create, the author continued, "Since the computer cannot handle infinity, it will be enough to calculate 500 iterations and use the number 10^8 (instead of infinity) to generate the Mandelbrot set."[5]

The result of the mapped Mandelbrot images is beautifully complex designs and fractals, which I highly encourage you to search and observe for yourself. As Lisle so eloquently demonstrated in his work on fractals, human beings simply discovered these mathematical laws over time but did not make them themselves. To that point, he wrote, "To discover something, it must already exist in a form that is 'covered' to us so that it may be revealed as we 'dis-cover' it." He continued,

> Laws of mathematics existed before the human mind. The atheist assumes that the human mind evolved over time and that in the distant past there were no minds in the universe. Yet [the atheist] also assumes that the universe obeyed mathematical laws at that time. Being conceptual, mathematical laws require a mind. But the atheist believes that there is no mind governing the universe. The atheist worldview is inherently contradictory.[6]

There are endless examples of the physical world obeying conceptual laws, specifically when it comes to mathematics. Lisle later pointed out how Johannes Kepler's second law states that planets sweep equal areas in equal times. Seeing that the planets most certainly existed prior to the human mind, how could a nonexistent mind create a complex law the universe is bound to obey? Simply put, the universe displays clear and articulable purpose–evidence of a Purpose-Giver.

What I have found to be true is that human beings continually discover that which already exists and beautifully articulate their discoveries. But mankind refuses to address the obvious questions of who caused the existence of such discoveries. They offer nothing other than the oversimplistic and absurd notion that the complex universe simply exploded out of nothing, while some dare to suggest that alien life outside the boundaries of our knowledge caused what we observe. Yet the alien theory still begs the question, who created the alien? What is most scientific and painfully obvious for even the greatest detractor is that our advances in science have only served to solidify the evidence for a Creator.

Fractal beauty? Infinite numbers? Incomprehensible complexity? I'm sure it's just an accident, right? Denying reality is sheer stupidity. But as discussed in the chapter on truth, the greatest impediment to discovery and truly understanding the universe is the self. If we are in fact created, and if we do in fact have purpose, then we are accountable to something outside of ourselves, and self must be limited. Since pride prevents us from laying down self in service of another, people resist, rebel, and fight against the obviousness of reality with all their might. So it would seem that simple surrender can lead to a vastly greater understanding of the world around us. The simplicity of the Christian-Judaic worldview is that it begins with surrender.

The Higher Moral Authority

Western civilization, being predominately founded on a Christian-Judaic worldview, recognizes the necessity for imperfect man to surrender to a higher, perfect power. This worldview drives the moral understandings within society and fuels the education and development of our children. The founders were undoubtedly aware of and perhaps influenced by the concept of surrender when they repeatedly recognized the role of Providence in the creation of the nation and the defeat of the mighty British military during the Revolutionary War. It was also the Christian-Judaic foundation that led the founders to create a system of government, namely a constitutional republic, which places morality at the center of power versus any single person or group of persons.

The concept of morality as king undoubtedly arose from biblical counsel the founders were well familiarized with, indicating time and time again the failures of man and the vices he is prone to. The founders were without a doubt familiar with the lessons taught in the story of the great King David, who was referred to as "a man after [God's] own heart" (1 Samuel 13:14). Despite David being a heroic and valiant warrior king, he fell prey to human failure and sins, and required a moral authority to regulate his kingship. In 2 Samuel 12:1-15, after David committed adultery with Bathsheba and sought to have Bathsheba's husband killed, the prophet Nathan severely chastised David for his immoral failure. In essence, a religious leader held the powerful king accountable to the higher moral authority, clarifying that no form of earthly government is above the Creator's standard. In 2 Samuel 12:7-9, Nathan reminded David that all his power was from God–it had been given to him–and thus David would be held accountable. Nathan told David:

> Thus says the LORD, the God of Israel, "I anointed you king over Israel, and I delivered you out of the hand of Saul.

And I gave you your master's house and your master's wives into your arms and gave you the house of Israel and of Judah. And if this were too little, I would add to you as much more. Why have you despised the word of the LORD, to do what is evil in his sight?"

God's dealing with David was severe, as the reader can see in the verses and chapters that follow in 2 Samuel, but what most identifies with the topic of purpose is that there was intentional and purposeful meaning in the position of king that David occupied. And it was not the government that determined the moral standards, but rather the government's job to ensure that the moral standards already in existence (just as mathematical concepts already existed before man discovered them) were maintained and protected for the people. We see clearly that government has a purpose; government was in fact created by God for the purpose of order and protection, and it is only a moral Law-Giver and Purpose-Giver who can hold man accountable.

The founders recognized this thoroughly as they observed the failures of governments throughout history and their own experience in dealing with the English king. They specifically determined to correct this error and reestablish the higher authority as the unalterable standard by which government was held to its purpose. Having established that no single man or group of people would be the ultimate authority, they enshrined the concept of the American republic accountable to a constitution based on God's moral authority. They added additional layers of accountability by requiring the powers that did exist to be separated and accountable to one another, leading to our separate branches of government. The founders' creation of the American government was purposeful, intentional, exact, and accountable.

In October of 1798, John Adams wrote to the officers of the Massachusetts Militia's Third Division and explicitly conveyed moral necessity in government and the people's need to adhere to this truth. He acknowledged, as all the founders did, that history has taught us that people are uncontrollably prone to failure and vices such as greed, pride, evil, and more. In a portion of his letter, Adams wrote,

> Because we have no government armed with power capable of contending with human passions unbridled by morality and religion. Avarice, ambition, revenge or gallantry, would break the strongest cords of our Constitution as a whale goes through a net. Our Constitution was made only for a moral and religious people. It is wholly inadequate to the government of any other.[7]

A Warning on Deviation

Seeing that purpose can be observed in almost every area of study one ventures toward–whether math, science, geopolitics, government, philosophy, society, and many more–we must ask the question, "Why have we deviated?" Or perhaps more to the point, "Why have we allowed this disconnection from what made us great and provided so much freedom and wealth that America has enjoyed for generations?" It is worth noting that because the creation of the constitutional government was so precise and intentional, and because the founders realized that it would only exist so long as it governed, as Adams said, "a moral and religious people," it is crucial to recognize those who seek to undermine these truths. Understanding that the Constitution was created to hold mankind accountable, recognizing man's proclivity to wander far from truth, why then do we not wholeheartedly confront leftist ideologues and secular humanists that seek to destroy all that the founders have done?

It would seem ostensible that because the American republic has been and continues to be a beacon of hope and refuge for the entire world, we would be on guard for those who would attack our way of life. Where are the republic's sentinels? Where have the founders' spirits gone? Whom have they now embodied, making certain our nation's continuance? I propose that without a generation willing to arm themselves with knowledge and engage the enemy in apologetic warfare, we will simply cease to exist, and this must not be so.

To all who see the truth, you are accountable. To all who live in reality and do not convey its truth to those around them, you are responsible. Let us not be as the sleeping guard, who allows the enemy to slip into the castle grounds and wakes at daybreak to say, "I did not see them!" Let it be established without further debate: the enemy is here, they always have been, and our necessity for defense has never been greater. Perhaps if nothing else, the purpose of your life is to preserve truth as best as your individual gifting will allow, to give glory to God, and to humbly serve your fellow man.

Purpose, it seems, is not so elusive as we would readily proclaim, but rather it is difficult to face and foreboding to an untested generation.

Chapter 4

Pride

What is pride?

Is it a good thing or a bad thing? Can it be both? Pride, in its most negative connotation, has aggressively infiltrated this generation to our detriment, but what is the root cause of this pedestaling of emotions? In this chapter, we'll discuss the Christian-Judaic perspective on pride and how the individual is supposed to view this emotion through the Christian-Judaic worldview. By contrast, we will also explore how the secular worldview predominantly sees pride and how it has affected our culture today.

Fact or Feeling?

I wonder if Ben Shapiro realized how popular his now famous quip "Facts don't care about your feelings" would become when he coined it all those years ago? The statement, however entertaining, is powerful in its own right. What Shapiro clarified in the simplest of forms is actually a biblical truth that has endured through the ages: emotions are fleeting and do not equate to facts. In essence, feelings are nothing to base decisions upon or anything that carries grave importance, because they rarely align perfectly with reality. Emotions are an intangible sense; they overtake rationality within the best of us and must therefore be tamed. Why? Because emotions, besides being so effervescent, are deceptive; they lie to you.

Take, for example, the most common of negative emotions: anger. There is perhaps no one who understands the ill-considered actions that often follow submission to anger's jurisdiction in a conversation more than a husband and wife caught up in the emotions of a sudden argument. The two, in an otherwise loving relationship, will hurl unheard-of insults at one another over petty disagreements that are not long remembered after the anger subsides. Pride, being a close friend to anger, becomes the only driving catalyst in the moment. Anger isolates its victim, disengages them from reality, and blinds their otherwise capable decision-making process. Taking any insignificant disagreement into mind, we must admit that an angry response indisputably accomplishes nothing. The feud is not quenched by berating the person you care about; in fact, it only worsens the situation. Anger and insult do not assist the other person, as the rage-blinded individual stupidly believes. Pride only serves to gash and disservice those closest to us and injures an already damaged circumstance.

The wise individual would momentarily ignore their emotions and evacuate themselves to rightly sort through their thoughts and feelings. Taking a moment to do something as simple as thinking (meaning replacing emotion with rational thought) about your situation and examining the veracity of the emotions clouding your thoughts will generally lead to a completely different adjudication of the circumstance, regularly resulting in self-realization and apology. Other emotions are equally blinding and deceptive. When combined with anger, jealousy, or doubt, pride becomes an intoxicating cocktail that inhibits even the highly tolerant from appropriately functioning.

If emotions are remarkably deceptive, why do we so often rely on them for the most important decisions of our lives? The imprudent and emotional person will consult feelings to choose where they work, who they date (or worse, who they marry), and perhaps even what matters most in life: what they believe about the world around them. They thereby allow fleeting, untethered emotions to dictate the course upon which they embark. While every important decision we make in life deserves the utmost attention and critical thought process, far too often emotions take command. Our culture today has made emotion king; this allows pride its full spectrum of negative influence.

If you were to ask the secular humanist today what they believed the concept, application, and meaning of pride were, you would most likely receive a confusing bag of loosely defined concepts that appeal only to the relativist. The secularist believes that self is to be exalted above all, and therefore pride is at the core of all decisions, guiding their every step. Needless to say, the secular man's concept of pride is at odds with the Christian-Judaic worldview of the same.

Pride: The Leftist's Worldview

Today's leftist will claim that there is in fact no greater source of wisdom than the feeling of fulfilling one's every whim and desire. That feeling drives and motivates their decisions and will not be hindered by what they proclaim to be outdated notions of humility and absolute truth. We see this publicly displayed at every turn, where self-gratification is the crowning achievement of the sentient humanists, who believe themselves absolved from the answerability of a Creator. Why? Because, as we earlier discussed, the worship of self is central to the cult of secular humanism. When pride replaces God, when God is notionally and culturally dead, as Nietzsche so eloquently described in his madman parable, the only deity left to cling to is self. Is there anything more prideful than individuals who view themselves as gods? Whether they say so or not, the leftist's ideological struggle to replace the God they cast aside leads to only one option: self-deification, which is the embodiment of pride.

But how have I arrived at this conclusion? Let's take a look at the ideological underpinnings of the humanist's culture. Theirs is a relativist culture that encourages the individual to "do whatever makes you feel good" or to "do what's right by your definition," no matter the consequence upon others. They deny the existence of absolute right outside of the individual's desire. This method of conducting oneself is detrimental to everyone involved. These individuals are unwittingly making themselves victims of their own pride, often hurting those around them. Herein lies the danger: if nothing and no one can press truth upon another, and the leftist has rejected the notion of absolute truth, then the self becomes the author and determiner of all the individual views as real. If the self is the author of all that is true, then no one outside of that individual has the right (or the ability) to challenge that person's belief in any way, shape, or form. Hence, today you see leftists out-virtue signaling one another in a confusing battle of idiocy as they vie for control of Virtue Hill.

One man who used his pursuit of self, or fulfillment of "True Will" as Aleister Crowley would put it, to greatly impact leftist politics is Saul Alinsky. Alinsky was a community activist, a communist, and considered by many to be an American version of Joseph Goebbels, the notoriously evil Nazi propaganda chief, for his proclivity to clone propaganda techniques of the likes of Hitler, Stalin, and Mao.

Hitler, for example, wrote in *Mein Kampf* that propaganda "must confine itself to a few points and repeat them over and over again." Alinsky, in like manner, wrote in his work *Rules for Radicals* that the organizer "dedicated to changing the life of a particular community must first rub raw the resentments of the people of the community; fan the latent hostilities of many of the people to the point of overt expression."[1] The idea Alinsky is expressing here is to keep messaging relevant and focused on key points repeatedly until they have been accepted as reality. Sound familiar? One can find similar tactics employed by Stalin and other radically dangerous dictators. But why the similarity? Why would Alinsky mimic the evilest of men that society has yet produced? I suggest it is because the source of the message is in fact a lie, driven by pride and in enmity against reality and truth itself. It takes a great deal of working to convince someone they do not exist; it only takes a pinprick to convince them they do.

No one is _____ (fill in the appropriate identity group) enough. There is always a more oppressed, a more marginalized, a more undervalued people. The irony of this perspective is that each group competing for ultimate victimhood is self-identifying. Thus there is absolutely no rational way to determine the veracity of any particular claim to victimhood. What's more, if you dare to challenge this backward and unintelligent method of thinking, you strike a blow at the person's most sacred core: their pride. This is an unforgivable secular sin.

No anti-Christian-Judaic adherent displayed this self-exalting philosophy more powerfully than Aleister Crowley. Crowley, founder of the occult spiritual philosophy known as Thelema, claimed to have received what he called *The Book of the Law* from a noncorporeal spirit named Aiwass, whom he described as a "tall dark man in his thirties . . . whose dress suggested Assyrian or Persian."[2] Keep in mind, Crowley said this "demon" spoke to him by channeling through his wife, Rose, while in Egypt on their honeymoon. And what exactly did this spirit with "deep timbered voice . . . and solemn tones" say to him while possessing his wife? Among many sayings outlined in Crowley's work, one specifically was of telling importance to this text: "'Do what thou wilt' shall be the whole of the law." Did you catch that? *Do whatever you want to do*. That's the entirety of what the individual should abide by—the quintessential embodiment of pride.

Crowley's demonic philosophy, however, is not the first time we've heard this message of self-exultation and pride. The first time, as discussed in length in the chapter covering purpose, was in the Garden of Eden and the story aptly named the Fall of Man. When Satan, much like Crowley's Aiwass, possessed and took the form of a serpent and spoke to Eve, he proposed one singular concept leading to the fall of humanity: do whatever you want, and you will become like God. The secular humanist persists in pursuing this concept—through failure, through defeat, through violence and death, through the worst human rights violations the world has ever seen brought on by the exaltation of self and the denial of truth; the leftists believe themselves higher than the Creator. That is pride.

Pride: The Christian-Judaic Worldview

So then, what is the correct perspective on pride? How should we tame the innate desire to lord over those in authority and make ourselves higher than God Himself? Can we, in light of humanity's repeated failures, attain peace amid a constant battle of the will? The short answer is, in and of ourselves, no. But, what if the individual looks to the Creator of life itself? Looking to someone outside the earthly and finite confines of humanity, what then?

Looking beyond the capacity of man is exactly what the founders of the American republic referred to when they created the United States. They acknowledged the dangers of pride, in all its forms, and, recognizing the failures that preceded them, established a very different venture. For the Christian, and primarily all of early Western civilization, the antipodal position to pride was only found in one source: the belief in the person of Jesus Christ. We see this over and over again in historical writings, monuments, and personal and governmental records. The United States Capitol area is covered with references to biblical Christianity and God's involvement in the formation of the nation.

In 1785, students of Yale College were instructed to "above all, have an eye to the great end of all your studies, which is to obtain the clearest conceptions of Divine things and to lead you to a saving knowledge of God in his Son Jesus Christ."[3] Benjamin Franklin, who described himself as a Deist, strongly touted the value of Christian-Judaic beliefs in the formation of the republic, as noted in *Benjamin Franklin: An American Life*: "[Franklin] retained a strong faith in a God as the wellspring of morality and goodness in man, and as a Providential actor in history responsible for American independence."[4]

Franklin, in his work *Articles of Belief and Acts of Religion*, wrote, "It is that particular wise and good God, who is the Author and Owner of our system, that I propose for the Object of my praise and adoration."[5] And if there was any doubt concerning Franklin's perspective on the sin of pride, he wrote himself a series of virtues that he held as true. Franklin listed thirteen virtues, one of which particularly dealt with man's pride. He carried these written virtues in a small book wherever he went, and concerning pride, he defined its opposite: "Humility: Imitate Jesus."

In summation, there was perhaps no greater example of the founders' clear belief in Christianity's influence and God's providing hand not only in winning the American Revolution but in establishing the republic and its founding documents than Franklin's speech at the Constitutional Convention on June 28, 1787, which included these words:

> We have gone back to ancient history for models of Government, and examined the different forms of those Republics which having been formed with the seeds of their own dissolution now no longer exist. And we have viewed Modern States all round Europe, but find none of their Constitutions suitable to our circumstances. . . .
>
> I have lived, Sir, a long time, and the longer I live, the more convincing proofs I see of this truth that God Governs in the affairs of men. And if a sparrow cannot fall to the ground without his notice, is it probable that an empire can rise without his aid? . . .
>
> We have been assured, Sir, in the sacred writings, that "except the Lord build the House they labour in vain that build it." I firmly believe this; and I also believe that without his concurring aid we shall succeed in this political building no better.[6]

May we learn to lay pride aside and humbly seek the Creator as the nation's founders did once upon a perilous time.

Chapter 5

Self-Defense

What is the Christian-Judaic perspective on self-defense?

How has Western civilization fashioned itself a truly unique definition of defending ourselves and those we love the most? In the following paragraphs, we will discuss the modern concept of self-defense, how it applies to the American republic, and how it is not only morally compatible but morally necessary. Besides the obvious emphasis on self-defense in a variety of contexts, whether physical or legal, the idea was something the American founders certainly thought of with the utmost gravity. Why? Perhaps because of the vast amount of suffering the world and they themselves had experienced due to an explicit lack of ability to protect themselves from individual threats and government overreach. Regardless, the founders were categorical: you have the right to defend yourself from another person and, more importantly in their minds, from the government. The Second Amendment, which grants the right to bear arms, only served to codify an existing belief.

Where Did the Need for Self-Defense Come From?

In the biblical story of Cain and Abel, an exemplary demonstration of pride and hate, we see the first murder of a human being.

Cain, upset with his brother and jealous of God's favor upon him, murders Abel. We know there weren't any firearms at this time, so perhaps the murder weapon was a wooden club or a rock, or even his own bare hands. Now, whether or not Cain considered his weapon an "assault" club, an "assault" rock, or "assault" hands is utterly irrelevant to the motivation that emanated from his uncontrolled emotions. The evil in Cain's heart overcame his emotions, which overcame his physical control. Acting upon those irrational feelings and thoughts, he murdered his brother.

God knew Cain's heart, and in Genesis 4:6-7, the Creator confronted Cain concerning the condition of the evil in his heart: "Why are you angry, and why has your face fallen? If you do well, will you not be accepted? And if you do not do well, sin is crouching at the door. [Sin's] desire is contrary to you, but you must rule over it." In the very next verse, Cain murders his only brother, Abel.

What strikes me most about these verses is God's warning of the power of sin and hate in a person's heart. God, being the embodiment of love, called to Cain even amid Cain's evil intentions and attempted to bring him into the fold. These verses specifically highlight mankind's necessity to "rule over" the evil desires of the heart at the obvious peril of losing control and committing violence upon others. What a powerful harbinger of things to come.

By the time we reach the twentieth century, human beings have taken evil to a grotesquely new level. It is a well-established fact that more human beings died in the twentieth century alone than in the previous nineteen centuries combined. Conservative estimates put the death toll at 100 million by leftist governments alone,[1] but if you consider additional secular governments such as fascist (another 28 million) and others, the number is much higher. Concerning genocide and government mass murder, R. J. Rummel, Professor Emeritus of Political Science at the University of Hawaii, argued that the number of dead was possibly 169 million in the twentieth century alone. It is simply astounding that despite these numbers so readily available to the critical thinker, we still have people walking around considering religion the catalyst for all violence and wars. While there may have been some manipulated form of religion by which evil men based evil actions, they pale in comparison to what anti-theist humanists have done.

This is a fearful truth, but it begs the question: Why? There is a direct and provable correlation between the most violent century in the history of the universe and mankind's unwillingness to act upon the wisdom of Genesis 4:7, in which God warned Cain, "But you must rule over it"–"it" being sin, "it" being evil desires and hatred, "it" being uncontrolled anger. What is so notable is the correlation between the previously mentioned evil, hatred, and uncontrolled anger and their source: pride. Man is under daily constraint to tame the self, to rule over it, to control the otherwise impossibly dangerous impulses that drive violence and irrational behavior.

And so, due to man's historical violence and proclivity to injure, maim, and kill his fellow man, we see from the earliest of times the requirement to defend and protect ourselves and those we love. The Western perspective is premised on the Christian-Judaic belief that mankind has intrinsic value and is created in the image and likeness of God, by God, for a specific purpose; therefore human life is worth defending.

America's Concept of Self-Defense

The Christian-Judaic answer to evil is simple: live by the teachings of Jesus. When Western civilization truly flourished, her ideals were able to defeat worldwide-accepted cultural norms such as slavery because of her Christian-Judiac values, not the opposite. The West's success can be attributed primarily to a homogenous culture of societal submission to a higher power, as revealed in the Bible. Because the Bible so appropriately identifies the very core of man's issues and prescribes a remedy, it became a highly relied-upon foundation on which to construct the American republic. The potency of biblical impact on a society is demonstrated, if in nothing elsc, by the severity of leftist attacks on Christianity; they know how effective the Church can be.

The founders recognized the necessity to control "the natural proclivity of man"; Benjamin Franklin often alluded to the vices of men and their proclivity for corruption and evil if left unchecked. During the Constitutional Convention of 1787, Franklin noted, "Sir, there are two passions which have a powerful influence on the affairs of men. These are ambition and avarice; the love of power, and the love of money. Separately each of these has great force in prompting men to action; but when united in view of the same object, they have in many minds the most violent effects."[2]

Of course, having the might of the world's largest military force knocking at their doorstep, the founders were keenly aware of what uncontrolled power could initiate. Jacques Mallet du Pan, a journalist and political leader who listened to Franklin's teachings while he was America's ambassador to France, wrote in his memoir that Franklin believed "whoever should introduce the principles of primitive Christianity into the political state would change the whole order of society."[3] We see that Christian-Judaic values and beliefs about the state of mankind and what to do about it would have inevitably supported most, if not all, of the early decisions concerning the American republic; this emphatically includes the concept of self-defense and the right to bear arms.

We can see clear examples of this in the way the founders and others lived their lives. Jonathan Trumbull was the British-appointed governor of Connecticut and a strong supporter of American independence. He exemplified a peaceful Christian and moral figure while simultaneously believing strongly that individuals had the right to resist tyranny and defend themselves. For example, he wrote in 1770 that people should pray that God "graciously pour his Spirit out upon them" and asked for a revival of the "peaceful religion of Jesus Christ." Simultaneously he, being a great friend of George Washington, contributed "large amounts of [fire]arms, munitions, and supplies" to further fight for American independence.[4] What is perhaps even more notable, given today's state of political ideology, is that Trumbull, in a governmental position and in official capacity, regularly called for people to pray and fast, asking God and Jesus for assistance and moral guidance.

In one instance, when writing to the English "Board of Trade," Trumbull declared that man had no true governor or master "but Jesus Christ." In 1775, Governor Trumbull officially proclaimed a Day of Fasting and Prayer for the Connecticut Colony, in a desperate appeal to God for providential guidance in the American fight for independence. But Trumbull was not the only governmental representative to call for official prayer and fasting. Thomas Jefferson, in response to British aggression against the American colonies, "drafted a Resolution calling for a Day of Fasting, Humiliation and Prayer" for their sister colony of Massachusetts.[5] With the assistance of Patrick Henry and others, the resolution passed in the Virginia House of Burgesses unanimously. And yet again, we see very early examples of both moral resoluteness and the concept of self-defense intertwined perfectly in righteous harmony.

And so in early American culture we see a notion of self-defense intricately woven into America's moral fabric as prescribed by Christian-Judaic beliefs. The founders laid the groundwork for the American concept of self-defense and the eventual Second Amendment, which even then was solidified in the hearts and minds of early Americans. What is unequivocal by the founders' actions is that, when given the opportunity to equalize the playing field, they resolutely ensured that every citizen of the United States of America would have the ability to arm themselves at equal capacity to the government that served them. This is inarguably the premise of the American concept of self-defense: protection from individuals and protection from ruling authorities if needed.

Self-Defense: Rooted in the Value of Human Life

You may have a grasp on Christian-Judaic American foundations, and separately on the concept of self-defense, yet still wonder how exactly they relate to one another. The answer lies squarely in understanding the value of human life. The secular humanist, and by and large the leftist political perspective, says, "You came from nothing, and nothing happens when you die," which absolutely reshapes their motivations and understanding of human purpose.

Not always to an extreme but certainly often enough for history to make note of it, secular humanist governments (that is, those who reject the notion of a Creator and life after death) have led the pack in extreme death and murder rates over the last few centuries. When confronted by this haunting historical fact, they only bring themselves to say things like "They weren't doing it right," while believing they can correctly implement what all others before them have failed to. The greatest examples of secular humanist governments have ended in horrifying tragedy and great human suffering.

Take, for example, the adherents of socialism, communism, fascism, Maoism, and so on (which I will henceforth refer to as the "isms"). What group among them can claim to have bettered the lives of those around them? Who among these "isms" governments can accurately say their system worked? Was it secular humanism that lifted vast portions of the world's population out of poverty? Absolutely not, it was capitalism. But the excuses are endless. Often you will hear the likes of "If the other countries would have let us" and "Capitalism quenched the fires of communism" or "The Western oppression prevented us from succeeding." These are just excuses, worth no more than the Soviet cash you may find in a museum.

The humanist's excuse for the inefficiency of their ideology is childish, and frankly very dangerous. If you are truly searching for the Achilles' heel of those "isms" systems, look no further than their abandonment of reality, hatred of individual accountability, and rejection of absolute truth in which the value of human life is grounded. It goes without saying those "isms" governments were not known for their care of the individual. From the iconic raised fist symbol of rebellion and communal-based worth to the eradication of millions of people unwilling to conform to their particular political ideal, the "isms" leaders were–and continue to be–savagely violent and evil because, in their rejection of God, they have rejected the value of human beings.

Launched from the premise of an evolutionary life view, the value of the individual and consequently the concept of life are completely diminished. As mentioned earlier, the "isms" leader will say, "You came from nothing, and nothing happens when you die"; hence, the only thing that matters in this life is the exaltation of the only power they are willing to acknowledge: government. When government is god, no man is safe, for the government itself becomes the determiner of right and wrong, the arbiter of safety and self-defense. It follows then that when you deify a group of individuals, their protection is of utmost importance. If their protection is of utmost importance due to their deistic status, then anyone who threatens what they say or do becomes by their own definition evil; and evil, after all, is worth fighting, is it not?

Speaking at an event in New York during her failed presidential campaign, Hillary Clinton famously stated that those who were not voting for her (specifically, half of those who supported her opposition) were "deplorable," thereby ostracizing and demonizing hundreds of millions of Americans who would be voting that cycle. So throughout history the Left specifically has found great value in demonizing those who oppose them. When all else has failed, the primary method of eliminating those who threaten the deistic powerhouses of the secular humanist, also known as "people who disagree with them," is to disarm them. Carefully note that history has shown this again and again: disarming citizens is a key milestone on the path to great tyranny.

But how can disarming a people be understood in conjunction with the value of human life? Simply put, you cannot reach the mass justification of forcefully eliminating your enemies without first convincing your followers that some lives are worth nothing. It starts slow and ends in final solutions. It is important to understand that the "isms" leaders do not win debates by rational or critical thinking. Theirs is a failed ideology that repeatedly turns on them like a rabid dog. Perhaps most telling of this fearful reality is the compilation of horrific stories illustrated in *The Gulag Archipelago* by Aleksandr Solzhenitsyn. His work is an eerie depiction of the "isms" years between 1918 and 1956 in Russia and its surrounding victim countries. In 1918, the Soviet leaders demanded the mass surrender of weaponry from its people. The penalty for noncompliance was ten years in prison. Of course, it goes without saying that loyal members of the communist party were permitted to retain their firearms. Solzhenitsyn eloquently said, "Unlimited power in the hands of limited people always leads to cruelty."[6]

Similar examples of this disarming ideology can be found in Maoists, South American dictators, Nazis, and so on, for the entirety of "isms" history and much of human history before them. The exception was and remains: the United States of America. It is woefully frightening that political entities in the United States have now fully adopted this anti-American ideology of disarming citizens. No alternative to the suffering that ensued in times past should be expected if they succeed in doing so.

In Mao's case, the elimination of political dissidents was absolutely necessary for political gain. Mao famously said, "Every Communist must grasp the truth, 'Political power grows out of the barrel of a gun.'"[7] It follows that forcibly eliminating your enemies is much simpler when you disarm them. Under Mao, the Nationalist government of China established strict gun control in 1935, then proceeded to murder over 65 million people in an attempt to create his Chinese socialist utopia.

What is it that unites the "isms" leaders on the Far Right and Far Left sides in their pursuit of disarmament? Despite vast differences between them, socialists being far to the left of fascists, they are united in their humanist belief that there is no ultimate accountability outside the power of the government. The socialists, like their cousins the fascists, believe that human life is not valued individually but rather in the greater good of the group. Any student of history can see this over and over again in the mass sacrifice of human life offered by "isms" leaders, directing their followers to death in order to achieve the political power they desire. From Soviet soldiers being sent into battle without weapons to Hitler's relentless murder of Jews in Europe, the value of human life is seriously depreciated under humanist ideologues. And why wouldn't it be? After all, you came from nothing, and nothing happens when you die, right?

In the moments of history just prior to all-out war, we see common precursors in all the "isms" movements: the mass collection of data and political information against the devalued human group (usually political dissidents or targeted people groups), the disarming movement, the mass elimination of life (preborn or otherwise), and so forth. One sure indicator of impending tyranny you are bound to identify in history is the devaluation of human life.

The Exception

In comparison to the "isms" leaders of the past, the Christian-Judaic worldview demands acceptance that life is sacred because God created it, not because man values it. Man, with all his failures, is removed from the equation, and an eternal Being sets the standard. The founders knew this; the founders believed this; and thus the reality of American exceptionalism was born.

When life is sacred, it is your inalienable right to defend it. It is your right to defend yourself, your family, your loved ones, your property, and your country. Anyone–and I don't say this lightly or without thought–who seeks to dismantle your ability to, at a minimum, equally oppose their ability to use force against you should be identified as anti-American, anti-Western civilization, and anti-Christian-Judaic values.

America was the exception to what previously was the historical norm: millennia of failed government types, evil dictators, and violent societies. As a republic established on the principles found in the Bible, America completely altered the course of history. Western civilization drastically improved the lives of millions of people and, though not without its failures, had a source upon which to judge evil unlike governments before it.

When those within our own family sought to propagate slavery, Americans died by the hundreds of thousands to defeat this evil because they believed in the biblical absolute truth of the value of human life. When Nazis nearly destroyed all of Europe, Americans fell upon its shores by the thousands, bringing freedom to all who would have it and then turning around and handing the land and nations back to the rightful owners–an unprecedented example of Christian-Judaic ideology abroad. Still to this day, when natural disasters strike foreign lands, America sends her support to the tune of millions of dollars, medical aid, supplies, manpower, and so on. The West is the last bastion of freedom and an example to the world. If America fails, the world fails. This reality brings a whole new perspective to every election, large or small, that each of us has the duty to participate in.

There is perhaps no greater initial foundation we must preserve than our right to defend ourselves and bear arms. This will be among the first group of rights our enemies seek to take from us. The Second Amendment is emphatically our right to keep the government accountable and to defend those we love. Self-defense is rooted in the biblical concept of life and the American concept of rights as established by the founders, who recognized the inextricable connection between successful government and acknowledgment of absolute truth. Near to the First Amendment's right to free expression, the Second Amendment ensures the remainder exist.

What is perhaps most shocking, given today's political climate, is that this concept needs to be reiterated–as if this were not the belief Americans have held for centuries. So why then do we struggle with what has so often failed the world in recent history? Because while Americans enjoyed their barbecues and pools on Memorial Day, her enemies infiltrated every aspect of American culture and, in Gramsci style, rotted her institutions from the inside out. Thus a new era is upon the American republic: a time when previously slumbering citizens must awake and take hold of the God-given right to self-govern, holding those in power accountable for their actions. Elections matter and voting matters; those who say otherwise have played into the enemies' hands. Exercise your options, take a stand, get involved, and don't allow the mistakes of the past to afflict their terrible damage on yet another generation of unsuspecting people.

Never let them take your ability to equally meet the government's force with your own. This is about accountability and not allowing room for temptation to take hold in the halls of power. This is about never letting the conflict start to begin with, and stopping any notion of sadistic, power-hungry leaders from conceiving a plan to strip citizens of their God-given rights. This is the United States' Second Amendment; this is America. Without it, we fall.

Chapter 6

Gender

What is gender?

Despite the battle currently being waged over whether or not there are 27,000 types of genders, the reality of the circumstance is indisputable: there are only two. A person can understand this without any outside education or manipulation of any sort; it is painfully clear. The absolute truth concerning gender is that human beings have distinct roles to fill within the binary context of their natural gender, and to trivialize the tremendous and powerful role of each individual man or woman is a grave mistake. When these roles are neglected for the pursuit of selfish desires, society suffers. However, neglecting these roles most certainly serves a political purpose, especially for the anti-theist seeking to undermine what made America exceptional to begin with and to overthrow the Christian-Judaic foundations of our republic in order to replace it with a new foundation built by an old foe: human secularism.

Don't Let Them Have the Children

One poignant question to begin the discussion on gender is "Why does the Left go after the kids?" It seems you can't view any media these days without seeing children at the epicenter of the raging gender battle. Whether in schools or on media designed for a child consumer, children have become the target of the sex cult in America. There was a time when children were considered sacred, untouchable, off limits to the political filth that saturates election cycles. That time has passed. While children are under assault by leftists at an earlier age than ever before in our country's history–by many ways and means, covering a variety of topics–there is perhaps no effort more damaging than the Left's over-sexualization of children.

Recently the retail giant Target suffered a $12.4 billion market value loss according to Fox Business as of June 12, 2023 (an amount that continues to rise), after stocking sexually oriented transgender clothing marketed to toddlers during pride month in 2023. This clothing, among other items, included homosexual pride-themed onesies and rompers sized for newborn babies. The trans clothing marketed to older ages included "tuck-friendly" swimwear, designed for men to "tuck" their penis so as to appear as a woman, and other items with slogans such as "Super Queer." I am shocked at the level America has descended to, specifically that corporations aim their transgender propaganda toward children.

Recently, and to our shame, we have seen story after story, headline after headline, about children subjected to transgender striptease shows, where grown men perform sexually provocative dance routines in front of young children. Many of these sexually charged molestations are conducted at public venues such as schools and libraries, and often at the taxpayers' expense. Children are equally subjected to sexual abuse by teachers and educators within public systems that require or encourage them to read books filled with pornographic images of abhorrent sexual acts and confusing gender propaganda. Our public education system now encourages rebellion against parents, reassigning the role of instilling "morality" from the parent to the state. They openly advertise that *only they* are "safe places," yet in these alleged safe havens, children are sexually groomed without the consent of parents.

In 2022, a group called Drag Story Hour NYC received thousands in taxpayer dollars to perform sexually explicit shows in front of audiences including children as young as three years old. According to a *New York Post* article, "Since January, the group has organized 49 drag programs in 34 public elementary, middle, and high schools. . . . Since 2018, the group–previously known as Drag Queen Story Hour NYC, before changing its name early this year–has received a total of $207,000 in taxpayer cash."[1]

It's not only public institutions controlled by leftists that propagate this sexually deviant yet politically driven effort. American corporations have jumped headfirst into the waters of propaganda as well. As of the time of writing this book, almost every major American corporation has subjected itself to the agenda of Diversity, Equity, and Inclusion (DEI) requirements, which in general are Marxist goals manifested in corporate requirements. According to the October 21, 2019 edition of *Time* magazine, "In 2003, MIT professor Thomas Kochan noted that companies were spending an estimated $8 billion a year on diversity efforts."[2] One can imagine how those expenditures have grown significantly since then.

In like manner, Anheuser-Busch saw losses upward of $40 billion in market value in 2023 (according to the *New York Post* on August 28, 2023) after creating a beer can with an image of reputed transgender social media star Dylan Mulvaney (a man who attempts to appear as a woman by use of hormones, apparel, and surgical mutilation) printed on the side. In a blindingly idiotic business decision, Bud Light Vice President of Communication Alissa Heinerscheid said during an interview with the podcast "Make Yourself at Home" on March 30, 2023, that "representation is sort of at the heart of evolution, you have got to see people who reflect you in the work,"[3] by which she meant including transgender ideology in their marketing plan was the only way for the company to stay relevant. This decision, of course, had the opposite effect, as any person with common sense could have imagined. Yet the company remains a multibillion-dollar machine.

We have reached an untenable position in which socialist, anti-theist efforts are subjugating an unaware generation to their political will.

What began as leftists claiming that those who opposed them were "exaggerating" and falsely presenting a "slippery slope" perspective of moral decline, declaring they would never advocate for children to be exposed to such vile sexual content, has now become a full-blown, self-fulfilling nightmare of historical proportions. With the Left unable to conceal their true intentions forever, Americans have moved from tolerating behavior that society did not condone to fully supporting, propagating, encouraging, and demanding immoral behavior at the peril of being ostracized by an intolerant Left.

But why not live and let live? Because actions have consequences, and silence is implicit consent. Every action demands a reaction, and there is no escaping reality, whether physically or metaphysically. Our declining moral culture is proof of that. What began as the sexual revolution has developed into endangering one of the American republic's key institutions of sustainability: the family.

Because actions have consequences, those who take actions yielding negative results must be held accountable. At a minimum, they must be opposed, and their destructive actions must be contained. There was a time when the Left's argument hinged solely on the individual's freedom to act; this, America tolerated. If a man wanted to dress as a woman and fulfill some sexual deviance on the weekends, he was, and is, free to do so in America. But that is a far cry from forcing all of society to fully condone, encourage, and demand that every American bend to the will of a political religion that dominates the cultural space. Long have those adhering to a Christian-Judaic worldview warned of this danger, as from its onset it appeared to any sensible individual to be much less about the sexual orientation of a person and much more about their political orientation.

Where is freedom for the individual now? The secular humanist cares not for individual freedom. In fact, opposition to individual freedom is essential to the advancement of their cause, because when a movement is antithetical to common sense, individuals must be forced to comply. The Left's argument is no longer "Let me do what I want," because if the Left acknowledges that gender confusion issues are solely based on an individual's mental crisis, sexual desire, or "personal want"–because there is no physical pathology regarding transgenderism–they can no longer virtue signal and impress upon everyone else the lie that sexual deviance is an "inalienable" right, which if, given a physical pathology, it would be uncontrolled by the person. According to the World Professional Association for Transgender Health (WPATH), "Being transsexual, transgender, or gender non-conforming is a matter of diversity, not pathology".[4] So clearly, if sexual behavior is only a choice (which it is), it cannot be defended in light of its horrendous damage upon Western civilization. The damage it causes the family unit, and subsequently the nation as a whole, is irreconcilable with leftist ideological claims and must be answered for.

Leftists know this and have learned a lot given the past one hundred years of leftist failure around the world regarding how to communicate their agenda. But, if the argument is posited from an immutable perspective (i.e., my gender is fluid and ever-changing; I was born this way; I have no control, and thus my sanctity must be protected), then one cannot argue for accountability concerning its degrading effect upon the nation because it is not tied to a person's choice. What they have essentially done with their efforts is departed from the catalyst of political motivation to one of secular metaphysical requirement–an intangible ever-changing source of motivation for the leftist, and one they can manipulate and alter as needed. Notably, this is the realm of the Church, which by and large has fallen asleep in the light and allowed the world to define morality–a role that rightfully belongs to God.

This is why you now see the equating of sexual deviance with race, that is saying that the color of one's skin or their ethnicity is equally as sacred as how one chooses to conduct themselves sexually. The Left noted the power of the Christian-Judaic stance of solidifying the protection of rights based on unchangeable attributes, and they sought to manipulate this truth for their political gain. And so the Left disgracefully equates transgender mental illness and sexual deviance with the plight of slavery. This is a disgusting and immoral comparison that appears to have been wholly accepted by many anti-theists as a way to circumvent responsibility for the failures and natural consequences of their movement while advancing their political agenda by making use of individuals suffering from mental health conditions.

What I mean to say is, if you are just a person wanting to act a certain way, you have the freedom to do so. You also will suffer the natural consequences of whatever you choose to do. No one is exempt from the absolute truths of reality, including the truth that actions have consequences. Alcoholics will suffer their natural consequences; drug addicts will suffer theirs; and sexual deviants have throughout history suffered tremendously by way of societal degradation, venereal disease, the loss of family, the loss of status, and the list continues–not to mention the effect that sexual deviance has, when fully embraced, upon the moral structure of the family unit, which in turn affects the entire society. One institution at a time–this is how empires fall.

Even today, we see the hypocrisy of the Left exemplified in the odd case of a disease originally named monkeypox, now formally known as mpox, which came on the heels of the coronavirus outbreak. After years of government overreach and tyrannical lockdowns due to the COVID virus, which was created in a Chinese laboratory and funded in part by the National Institute of Health (NIH), they refused to acknowledge or take action against the emerging threat of mpox. Ninety percent of the mpox cases were found in homosexual men (and children they had contact with), yet the government refused to implement any type of restriction whatsoever on gay orgies, generally considered to be the most common method of contracting the disease. Critics on the Left pointed self-righteous fingers at those who indicated the obvious correlation between sexual behavior and the illness, claiming that to deny men their sexual orgies was homophobic, racist, and whatever other name they could think of to call those who opposed their perspective. The sheer idiocy of this hypocritical ideology should be evident for all, and their political intentions for doing so should be carefully noted. They imposed great suffering upon many for political reasons related to COVID despite evidence to the contrary, and yet when faced with a clearly definable disease emanating from a plainly obvious source, they did nothing. Why? Because it served no purpose to their political agenda.

Should Americans believe in individual freedom? Absolutely. Does individual freedom have limitations? Absolutely. You are free to self-destruct to a certain degree, but there are limitations to selfishness. Society can tolerate a limited number of selfish individuals who contribute nothing to their communities in the name of individual freedom, but it cannot handle an entire generation doing so. For example, a drunkard who is living on the sidewalk because he refuses to take any responsibility for his actions or stop drinking is free to live as he chooses. But that same individual must also reconcile with whatever his actions cause upon himself. It is plain to see that just because one has the freedom to drink himself into homelessness, that does not mean this should be taught as a positive behavior to our children in public schools. In like manner, one is free to conduct their sexual deviance, but no one should be required to wholeheartedly support and condone their behavior. Yet a narrative has carefully been woven to skirt the commonsense reality of it and manipulatively convince an entire generation that destroying one's society is somehow "freedom" and "loving."

Should society allow people the freedom to be drunks and alcoholics? To a certain extent, within limits, yes. The Christian-Judaic perspective demands it! Remember, it is the Christian-Judaic worldview that births the concept of freedom and individual responsibility. Freedom of the will is essential to Christian theology. Free will defines the Christian concept of God's love toward mankind. It by no means follows that we should desire an entire generation of drunk idiots living on the streets, or people using drugs, or others sleeping around with whomever they wish, casting aside the value of the family unit and never contributing to society. One can easily see how that would quickly become a problem. Imagine for a moment that every member of society chose to live out every fantasy and selfish desire of their heart. Imagine they indulged every whim that crossed their mind and fully dedicated themselves to the pursuit of pleasure. Who would put on the police uniform and respond to urgent calls for help? Who would put on the boots and drag the hoses to burning buildings? Whose steady hands would guide the scalpel in life-saving operations? Who would soberly take the reins of government agencies and lead the nation as statesmen? Who would put on the uniform and sacrifice their own lives for the freedom of others?

You see, not everyone gets to be selfish, or we all suffer for it. This is the primary difference between tolerance and condoning. Tolerance, simply put, is society's allowance of what we know to be wrong or disagree with because we hold individual freedom in such high regard. Tolerance, however, by no means equals condoning or full acceptance of detrimental behavior. This would be a lie–to deny individuals the truth concerning their negative actions–and would damage society as a whole.

So how have we come so far–from tolerance to full condoning? Have we forgotten all that is good? Have we lost our sense of rational thought? Will we not pay the price for such a foolish abandonment of common sense? Of course, I'm speaking in broad terms, but this broadly relates to a variety of societal and cultural issues. Redefining what is timelessly accepted as reality when it comes to gender is dangerous–just as dangerous as it would be to allow any vice to fully permeate society without expecting there to be consequences. And to augment the danger of completely ignoring reality, the Left has taken it one step further and decided to launch an all-out assault on the youngest, the unsuspecting, and the most vulnerable: our children.

Stop and consider this for a moment: Can a child who pretends to be a dinosaur one instant fully understand the consequences of chemical castration the next? Does the child who should be learning about math, science, art, and American history really need to learn about anal sex in public school? I argue emphatically that the Left's goal has never been with regard to the individual, but rather the pursuit of political power. Do the leftist elites, with their many mansions and millions of dollars, care whether or not transgender strippers are properly represented in government? No. Should we allow the sacrifice of our children's innocence upon the altar of failed immoral leftist politics? No. Where are the fathers? Where are the concerned mothers? Where is the Church? Why have we surrendered our children to the state?

Why Is Gender Political?

I submit to you this obvious truth: you are being deceived.

As you take a deeper look, you'll see that there is a purpose to every propaganda effort, and it's more nefarious than you imagine. There is a simple explanation for virtually every agenda advanced by the anti-theist, and it solely relates to their political goals. If America can be fundamentally changed from the inside out, then anti-American ideologues will have been successful in destroying what America once was and replacing it with what history has shown to be the greatest evil the world has ever seen. Their goal? The cult-like religion of secular humanism, manifested in the political ideals of Marx and implemented by violent authoritarians throughout the twentieth century. God is replaced by government, but rest assured their secular followers are just as, if not more, zealous in their adherence to their beliefs than any religious person alive today. It takes great dedication to one's belief system to knowingly pursue foolish and damaging objectives at the expense of the most vulnerable among us. Theirs is the manipulation and subjugation of an entire generation of American children, all for the sake of human secularism bent on fundamentally changing the United States and erasing our moral and Christian-Judaic foundations, no matter the cost.

Why should Americans oppose this movement? Because all of history has shown the manifestation of evil to appear in the form of secular humanist governments, hell-bent on eliminating the influence of godly men and eradicating biblical notions of morality in favor of the cult of self-worship. When an individual's behavior begins to negatively impact society, there are limitations. Just as you cannot scream "fire" in a crowded theater, you should not condone actions that lead to the destruction of society. But what actions would be so drastic as to lead to the destruction of society? Those actions that threaten the foundations upon which society is built. So it follows that if the family unit is essential to a strong society, which it indisputably is, then assaults on what constitutes a strong family–say, perhaps the male and female gender and their important roles in child development–are assaults on American society at large, and just one of many.

This moral fabric of America has long been acknowledged by her enemies as an impenetrable wall that defends and preserves the American geopolitical worldview, and more specifically Western civilization. Cleon Skousen, in his book *The Naked Communist*, poignantly outlined forty-five communist goals to turn America into a communist-socialist state. In his op-ed "The Naked Communist, 60 Years Later," William Haupt described Skousen's depiction of the communist strategy: "A key stratagem is to destroy the family to impair the bonding unity that creates and molds character and morality. This will also diminish their interest in Judeo-Christian religions."[5] Why would the communist be concerned about family strength, morality, and Christian-Judaic influence if in fact they did not pose a significant obstacle to the secular humanist's goals? Why would Leninism be concerned with the sexual nature of a society and its beliefs thereof? Because Lenin and many others like him recognized the unbeatable strength that America's moral fabric represented.

America's enemies watched Americans overcome great odds. They studied in history about Americans defeating the great British Empire in providential, miraculous manner. They watched

Americans, fueled by Christian-Judaic resolve, defeat slavery. They watched young Americans storm the beaches of Normandy against hellfire and certain death. They watched as Americans liberated concentration camps and freed captives. They watched as American democracy brought freedom to the oppressed. And they watched Americans do so willingly because Americans believed in something greater than themselves. The founders believed the biblical notion of wisdom being derived only from the fear of the one true God; it is there in the pages of God's revelation of Himself to His creation that one finds wisdom. Many are the intellectuals in government, but few are wise. This can only be attributed to the fact that they have long ago abandoned the only source of discernment in favor of the pursuit of self-exaltation.

For secular humanists who wish to usurp the American way of life in favor of a socialist state, these moral strengths–family being one of them–are a constant thorn in their side. The Christian-Judaic ideals of family, marriage, value, purpose, and even gender have unquestionably been tied to the country's strength and performance in times of adversity.

As a side note, when considering the great evils of the "isms" governments, as well as the extensive efforts taken by Americans to counteract their influence, it is utterly shocking and reprehensible to see them now openly advocated for by duly elected American representatives in our own government. That we as Americans have allowed our enemy's ideology to encroach so deeply into our political decision-making is extremely dangerous. When you see leftist politicians lauding the wonders of socialism–long recognized as contrary to the American form of government–and running political campaigns as actual socialists, remember what America's enemies themselves have said. Consider this quote from Vladamir Lenin, taken from his book *The State and Revolution*: "Socialism is just the lower phase of communism used to facilitate true communist puerility which is its highest phase. Karl Marx believed socialism was the easiest road to pure communism."[6]

I hope to impress on you the grave seriousness with which one should consider the source of cultural movements. As a citizen of a republic, when you observe mass cultural-propaganda efforts, especially those waged against children in our public schools and beyond, you should always consider the greater purpose and intention of those in control of the messaging.

There is really little to be said on the topic of gender itself, as it is such an obvious reality that only two genders exist. By comparison, there is much to be said regarding the effort to convince you otherwise–you should ask yourself why they are doing this.

Now, one may argue that a person "wants" to live like a different gender, and they may and should be free to do so in America. But Americans should be equally free to oppose this idiotic behavior and defend our children and our nation from the rot caused by the selfish sexual infatuations of grown adults. There is no constitutional guarantee that a person cannot be told they are wrong; the Left has a major problem with this truth. The secular humanists simply cannot abide a rational conversation that counters virtually any aspect of their ideology, because their ideology is insufficient when confronted by the critical thinker and falls apart at the slightest breeze of truthful air. And so, in turn, the secular humanists look to seize power by force and to use that force to silence their political dissidents. They utilize the often not-spoken-of branches of power within this country such as media, culture, the economy, and more to pressure, intimidate, and at times take violent action against those who dare to speak truth. Once in power, secular humanists force their illogical ideology on the masses and solidify their own power by controlling and eliminating their political enemies.

Can you truly say that leftist politicians care about the small percent of mentally struggling individuals who identify as transgender? Can you truly agree that there is no ulterior motive behind this massive effort to eliminate the Christian-Judaic influence in American society? Have you paused to consider the ramifications of this ongoing effort, which seeks to chemically castrate children and even, as California's Senate Bill 107 recently proposed, grant the government authority to seize and take custody of children whose parents refuse to participate in this gender-bending immorality? This is a cold war, not yet ignited by the spark of revolution, which is in fact the end goal of all socialist-communist efforts.

As noted in a previous chapter, Mao, during an emergency meeting of the Chinese Communist Party in 1927, said it best: "Every Communist must grasp the truth, 'Political power grows out of the barrel of a gun.'"[7] As Americans are now seeing, the Left tolerates all behavior from those aligned with their values, but none from their political enemies. The leftist hypocrisy and immorality know no bounds, yet they will lecture their political opponents on morals and ethics–actions that are laughable at best.

Taking into consideration the Left's larger goal of destabilizing a society in order to dominate it–to create chaos and seize power– one should carefully dissect every major cultural movement they support. And so, we now examine the alleged "transgender identity" movement, which has grown in influence and strength among a naive and uninformed youth. Make no mistake, those propagating it are well-educated and intending adults manipulating a younger generation for political purpose, without any consideration for the damage they are causing. That damage is not only to the individuals who become their victims but to the nation as a whole, as immorality weakens the family structure and the natural strengths of men and women. The entire public discourse surrounding gender in today's culture is unequivocally political in nature. It is manufactured and disseminated masterfully, like all leftist propaganda efforts, to yield political results. Just as the Left attempted to illegally frame the forty-fifth president of the United States on multiple occasions, through various staged issues intent on influencing his election, they now advocate for the identification and removal of children from parents who disagree with their vile anti-theist sexual infatuations–the common denominator being lies and political motivations.

The Christian-Judaic Response to Gender Confusion

As with any wrongdoing, the Christian is called to confront the wrongdoer with truth. Does this mean that Christians should hate those who disagree with them? Quite the opposite. To hate someone would be to condone behavior that is detrimental to that person. This is exactly what the secular world has done in mislabeling "love" as condoning behavior. Christians are to accomplish the opposite of hatred, which is, in contrast, to love someone by telling them the truth in an effort to save them from the natural cause-and-effect consequences of life, and from ultimate separation from God in eternity.

As covered extensively in the chapter on love, it is common sense that those who care most about an individual will do everything they can to prevent them from self-harm because they love them. It is the uncaring stranger who is more likely to allow a person to do whatever they want, no matter how bad or self-destructive the person's actions are, because the stranger does not love that person and does not care. The leftists have completely turned that simple truth upside down, and they propagate the lie that in order to "love" someone, you must in fact allow them to do whatever they want to do–uninhibited worship of self, no matter the cost or damage caused to themselves or those around them.

This ideology is foolish and naive. It is so disconnected from reality and so harmful to society that the damage it has caused is difficult to quantify. From record drug-overdose deaths to sexual mutilation of our youth in the trans community, the horrors of denying reality and calling it "love" are tragically evident. And so, it is the Christian's obligation to be truthful and therefore loving to their fellow citizens. As Americans, we should consider condoning behavior based on whether or not it has positive or negative results on our society and individual lives. Of course, for the Christian, this is simplified by the guidance provided by God Himself. Our guide, by which we measure behavior to be beneficial or not, is the Bible, which consistently and steadfastly correlates with reality.

This reliance upon biblical guidance is not, as the Left would paint it, the "rise of Christian nationalism" but simply the existence of successful American values prior to the attacks by its enemies, the secular humanists. This has always been what America is about: Christian-Judaic values upheld by citizens who believe inalienable rights come from God, not the government. Long did America rely on biblical guidance for societal standards; this is evident throughout all of our founding documents and history. The founders specifically noted that the person of Jesus was to be imitated in the conduct of American society. They believed that the imitation of Christ would lead to a positive and successful outcome for the great experiment called America.

As noted in the opening pages of *100 Bible Verses That Made America* by Robert Morgan, George Washington himself, in addressing the original thirteen governors of the newly formed United States in 1783, said,

> I now make it my earnest prayer, that God would . . . most graciously be pleased to dispose us all, to do Justice, to love mercy, and to demean ourselves with that Charity, humility and pacific temper of mind, which were the Characteristicks of the Divine Author of our blessed Religion [Jesus Christ], and without an humble imitation of whose example in these things, we can never hope to be a happy Nation.[8]

These words are a far cry from male strippers dancing for children at public schools at the taxpayers' expense. Perhaps this is why the leftists are so adamantly attempting to delete and distort any record of Christian-Judaic influence in this country, to erase the reality that the Bible's influence was crucial in the formation and subsequent strength of our nation. If they manage to do so, if they manage to convince an entire generation that our founders did not base every aspect of the American government on Christian-Judaic principles, then and only then can they make great strides in restructuring the foundations of America. If they are able to remove the historical reliance on biblical principles, they can make Christians enemies of the state. They are attempting to do so today at a faster rate than ever before, as they have targeted specific aspects of culture, like gender and family, and used these issues to turn the culture away from Christian-Judaic thoughts on those matters. By isolating citizens from the truth of where their nation truly came from and what the founders believed on these matters, the Left is able to reeducate and indoctrinate a new generation with secular humanist lies and seize power from those who oppose them.

Think it can't happen here? Why? Are we as a people not just as human as any other people group in nations where Christians have been persecuted and eliminated? Did not German pastor Dietrich Bonhoeffer challenge Hitler's evil and suffer execution for it? Did not Christians opposing the pagan evils of Nero's Rome suffer excruciating persecution at the hands of his violence? Did not every leftist, communist, or other "isms" secular government persecute Christians specifically? Why? Because truth matters. And if you are launching a secular political agenda on the premise of lies, Christians, as the arbiters of truth, pose a very real problem to you. The "isms" leaders must counter truth with their lies if they hope to be successful in their propaganda efforts and achieve their goals of a godless existence.

Specifically to the point at hand, the Left has manipulated the concept of gender to accomplish the division they require to seize power. By separating people along lines previously unimaginable within American society, they've convinced half the population that sexual deviance toward children should be accepted as normal and even good. As Christians we have the duty to confront these wicked lies whenever possible. The gender-confusion rage and sexual abuse of children (specifically in surgical mutilation efforts) occurring in our culture today are a political lie–a very dangerous lie, in many victims' own words, that has lifelong medical and psychological consequences, not to mention the consequences it has societally, upon the family structure and subsequent effects nationally. If we lose strong families, we lose strong individuals. If we lose strong individuals, our nation has no one on whom to entrust the preservation of the institutions that compose a first-world country, no warrior class on which to rely for the preservation of freedom, no trustworthy statesmen upon which to cast the heavy burden of geopolitical adversity. When faced with such a life-impacting issue, is it not the obligation of Christians to love people in truth? If Americans, once identified as members of a Christian-Judaic nation, don't confront lies that destroy the lives of our children, who will? One can clearly see the political motivation by leftists seeking to overthrow the American form of government hijacking children as pawns in their political war. Is it not every patriotic American's duty to resist sexually deviant movements, which seek to undermine our nation's greatest source of strength: the family? And if an American duty is apparent, how much more should the Christian, who holds the truth of eternal life and reality itself, be held accountable?

"How?" you may ask. Show up and vote. Run for office. Peacefully protest outrageous abuses of our children. Get involved wherever possible. We must employ every effort afforded to us in a constitutional republic to counter the lies and political assaults on our nation. Christians, of all people, should be at the forefront of this effort, leading the charge for truth, standing for what is right, and defending the weakest among us. How will a lost and confused world know the truth if you do not call to them? How will the blind see if you do not guide them? Are Christians not called to be the hands and feet of Jesus? Are you not by definition an ambassador? Darkness will only prevail so long as the light is kept off. Americans and Christians alike, you have a powerful light! Shine it upon your nation, and do not fear what repercussions may come. Apathy will be the death of us. In 2022 I attended the annual PragerU gala in Beverly Hills with my wife, Lindsay, where Dennis Prager sat down to converse culture-war issues with renowned psychologist Jordan Peterson. Prager, who is a conservative radio talk show host, writer, and cofounder of the wildly successful nonprofit organization

PragerU, said something during the discussion that I immediately wrote down: whoever considers themselves conservative today but rejects the biblical wisdom of God is simply running on the fumes of the Christian-Judaic influence of our founders. Prager was implying that we are in grave danger, as the metaphorical "vehicle" which is America is running out of fuel and will soon face a crisis. I agree, and if this is true, it means that we will not last much longer if we do not retrieve the mantle of truth borne by our forefathers and carry it boldly into the future.

Let us then boldly confront the lies of the enemy. Let us take absolute truth to the public square and proclaim, without fear, the consequences of bad behavior and the results of godless immorality. Let us protect our most valuable asset, our children, and defend them relentlessly. Let us love our fellow men by always being truthful concerning their behavior.

As Christians, if we do not fiercely oppose the lies of the enemy, specifically regarding those we are charged with protecting and entrusting our future to, no one else will. It is a shame which history itself bears witness to–when Christians shirk their God-given boldness in favor of apathy and comfort, great suffering ensues.

The LORD is my light and my salvation; whom shall I fear? The LORD is the stronghold of my life; of whom shall I be afraid? (Psalm 27:1)

Chapter 7

Marriage

What is marriage?

The single most important human relationship one can observe and learn truths about reality from is marriage. Marriage is the union of one man and one woman, a relationship and institution created by God to exemplify His relationship toward mankind and even His very nature. Other relationships may be valid to particular individuals or circumstances, but marriage is specific to God's definition. He made it; He owns the copyright. To the American and Christian alike, it is a sacred and holy institution that the world has continually desecrated with alternative definitions and practices.

Why is understanding the purpose of marriage so important in today's society? Because the way one lives out their marriage exemplifies greater eternal truths and instructs the generations that follow on the proper relationship of God and man, man and woman, citizens and their government, and children and their parents. Marriage is the premise and catalyst for a child's understanding of God's order, authority, structure, love, and sacrifice, and it serves as the foundation for effective nation-building.

Marriage: The Christian-Judaic Worldview

Have you ever wondered why divorce is so rampant in our society? Have you stopped to consider the consequences of these failed marriages on children and the burdens they carry into their own relationships going forward? Most, if not all, of God's biblical instructions regarding life and how we are to live it are derived from a sense of protection that God seeks for the world He loves. That is, it is usually the case that if God says to do or not do a particular thing, it is because He desires what is most beneficial for an individual, and His commandments come from a heart of love. Now take this concept of biblical protective guidelines into the context of marriage. I begin this section with the understanding that marriage as defined by God is the greatest form of relationship a man and woman can have. When properly conducted, marriage is a source of happiness and fulfillment that the world has long sought after but has not been able to find.

According to the Bible, marriage is an example of Christ's relationship to the Church. Isaiah 62:5 says, "For as a young man marries a young woman, so shall your sons marry you, and as the bridegroom rejoices over the bride, so shall your God rejoice over you." Ephesians 5:25-28 says,

> Husbands, love your wives, as Christ loved the church and gave himself up for her, that he might sanctify her, having cleansed her by the washing of water with the word, so that he might present the church to himself in splendor, without spot or wrinkle or any such thing, that she might be holy and without blemish. In the same way husbands should love their wives as their own bodies. He who loves his wife loves himself.

Jesus' dedication and ultimate sacrifice are an example to the husband of how to conduct himself selflessly in support of his betrothed. Marriage also exemplifies the character of God Himself. Two equally valuable but distinct individuals come together as one and complete a whole. When children are added, you have a third element of a marriage that comes together to form one entity: the family. Since God invented marriage, it is His to define and structure. The Christian-Judaic perspective on marriage is directly derived from the Word of God and His admonition on how to live it out. Unlike the trivial political perspective that seeks to undermine the value of its biblical definition, marriage is a sacred and holy institution that the Christian is therefore obligated to protect and strengthen.

Because we know that God's advice is beneficial to all areas of life, both personal and political, the same is true with marriage. If lived according to the biblical prescription, marriage is an incredible and beautiful union that benefits not only the individual person but also their family, those around them, and society at large. Everyone benefits from healthy marriages. There is less infidelity, less lying, less untrustworthiness, less scheming, less arrogance, less hatred, and less stress when there is a happy and healthy marriage at home. Generally speaking, a man and woman in a healthy marriage tend to be less selfish than single persons, as marriage demands a great deal from the individual; they have learned to lay down their personal desires for the benefit of others–especially when taking children into account.

Man's Role in Marriage

As noted earlier, Ephesians 5:25 says, "Husbands, love your wives, as Christ loved the church and gave himself up for her." Could there be a higher calling than to lay down one's life for another? This is the perspective that men have been called to embrace. In the context of marriage, men are to live their lives completely and utterly in service to their spouse. If married, a man's first and foremost ministry is his family. The Bible calls men to lead their families toward a godly understanding of life and to lead by example. Men have a unique and specific role to fill in the lives of those around them and, most importantly, in the lives of their family. Men, being genetically and indisputably different from women, are born with an innate desire to protect and defend, to uphold the weak, and to ensure the success of those they care about through sacrifice.

As is the case with everything the Bible commands, the concept of gender roles, specifically those in marriage, are inextricably tied to practical applications. The indisputable differences between men and women at a biological level are seen practically in the world all around us. Men by far represent the greatest number of deaths in wars and life-threatening jobs, such as law enforcement, emergency services, and the military. Additionally, men compose the population of the vast majority of labor-intensive jobs the world has to offer; this is not coincidental. Men are born with inherent biological characteristics, both physical and emotional, that set them apart from the only other gender that exists. The strengths of men are intentionally implanted to complement the strengths of women, with each gender filling the gap in one another's deficiencies so as to form a perfect entity in the institution of marriage. But, to fully appreciate marriage as God intended requires commitment, steadfast dedication to another individual, discipline, sacrifice of self, and lifelong devotion to a purposeful way of life.

In the context of marriage, a man's actions as a husband and father will translate into how the wife and children figuratively view God as a husband and father. A wife sees that a husband is to be an example of what Christ is to the Church, so then the husband bears a great burden to properly live that example out in a truthful and powerful way. The way a man treats his wife is the lens through which a wife (in the best case) will see her relationship with God. Likewise, when we teach our children about God as our Father, it is the concept of what a father is–the one they have learned from their earthly father–that will resonate in their minds concerning God's relationship toward them.

Of course, this is not without exception. These relationships are often poisoned by mistakes and the sin nature of mankind. I am not saying that marriage is the only way for a wife and children to see God in light of biblical truth; that would be foolish. It is more accurate to say that we are supposed to be this example in our individual roles, and in a perfect world this would always be the case. Yet, God works His purpose and love toward us all regardless of our failures; this much is reassuring. Just because we fail in our obligation to represent God in our relationships, it does not mean that God is unable to overcome this and restore a broken life. This burden is tremendous and worthy of a man's utmost attention. Husbands must first live out their faith before the ever-watching eye of their wife. If they fail in this regard, their claim of Christianity is worthless.

Societally speaking, men today have often failed miserably at the task of leading their families and communities. Caught up in every distraction imaginable, from sports games to hobbies to social media, too many men have retracted into childlike immaturity and left their wives and children floundering for assistance in a confusing world of moral decrepitude.

Avoiding Man's Proclivities
In order for a man to fully live out his potential and fulfill the role of husband and father, he must address issues men struggle with. Lust has long entrapped men and led them down paths of destruction and suffering. It is a vice that is sure to disable even the most honorable of men. Throughout time, the indulgence of lust has destroyed marriages, relationships, partnerships, even governments. It is beyond essential for a man to acknowledge susceptibility to lust and the sexual desire he is naturally born with. While sexual desire is natural and God-given, it is only truly fulfilling within the appropriate confines of marriage. Outside the institution of marriage, lustful behavior and sexual deviance only lead to suffering.

This is an important point to reiterate: sexual desires we are naturally born with do not automatically become justified by nature of existing. In other words, just because you are born a certain way, it does not justify you fulfilling your every whim and feeling. Men have a moral and societal obligation to dominate the self and exercise control over their emotions. It is an emphatic lie that if you are born with a certain proclivity, then you are justified in acting out your desires; quite the opposite is true. Being born with detrimental proclivities simply makes you human. It is the discipline of controlling the self that vexes mankind and points to our need for a saving grace. The secular humanist's mantra is in stark contrast to this reality. The secularist demands adherence not to a higher power but to every fleeting emotion that deceives man with temporary pleasure, ultimately costing him his life.

Take, for example, pornography. Once a scarcely available medium, pornographic material can now be accessed by men (and a growing number of women) at any given time with ease. Men must acknowledge this reality and confront it head-on, taking active steps to avoid its pitfalls. For the modern man and the Church itself, this is a challenge that demands attention.

Furthermore, it is only in full awareness of the enemy's tactics that a husband can defend his family from what culture seeks to weaponize against him. The massive sexual infatuation within our culture intends to destroy the Christian-Judaic family model. Film and media content over-sexualizes young children at an earlier age than ever before, and now the militant transgender movement supported by leftists in America is openly advocating for grooming young children for sexual conduct and exposure. As early as elementary school, young boys are accessing explicit sexual content. It is the responsibility of fathers and mothers alike to counter this existential threat to their families and our culture. But, how can a father stand up for his children against the threats of sexual immorality if he himself is a victim and willing participant of its evils? Men need to stand up for what is right and fulfill their natural role as protectors.

Man cannot fulfill his God-intended role unless he first holds himself accountable. Needless to say, sexual immorality has no place in a marriage. If you are a Christian man, uncontrolled passions will destroy your relationship with your wife and fundamentally change the way you feel and think about your marriage. Men need accountability. Every man should have an accountability plan. Churches, in acknowledgment of modern threats to marriage and man's relationship to God, need to hold men accountable, especially those serving within the context of ministry. Man up, do the right thing, and hold yourself and those around you accountable for actions you know full well are destroying our society.

How can you, as a man, righteously lead your family, your sons and daughters, into truth when you yourself cannot control the simplest of vices? How will weak men protect our children from the onslaught of sexual content in social media, where children are bombarded daily with the most perverse sexual notions imaginable? Men need to stop being cowards and instead hold fast to the truths of God. Men need to first hold themselves accountable before taking to the streets with their opinions of others, political or otherwise. Men need established networks of accountability from other men to ensure that they, as intelligent and mature individuals, are first addressing their weaknesses before going into proverbial battle.

In a wise warning to his son in the book of Proverbs, Solomon described the dangers of a man falling into the trap of lust and sexual deviance. Proverbs 5:3-6 says, "The lips of a forbidden woman drip honey, and her speech is smoother than oil, but in the end she is bitter as wormwood, sharp as a two-edged sword. Her feet go down to death; her steps follow the path to [hell]; she does not ponder the path of life; her ways wander, and she does not know it." And again in Proverbs 5:21-23, Solomon gave a warning to the man who lacks discipline in this area, who does not take steps to keep himself accountable: "A man's ways are before the eyes of the LORD, and he ponders all his paths. The iniquities of the wicked ensnare him, and he is held fast in the cords of his sin. He dies for lack of discipline, and because of his great folly he is led astray."

I am not attempting to claim that you should be a perfect sinless human in order to seek righteousness and be a good husband and father. On the contrary, I am saying that the beginning of the journey to become those things starts with acknowledging the reality of your fragility; any man who tells you he doesn't ever struggle with sexual temptation is a liar. The best way to deal with anything that affects your relationship with God and your marriage is to openly confront it and take measures to prevent it from being a problem in the first place. This goes for most issues men struggle with: infidelity, greed, selfishness, anger, drug and alcohol addiction, etc. A wise man will first acknowledge who he truthfully is in light of reality (fallen and in need of a Savior) and then look to God for the power to overcome the wickedness of this world, taking heed lest they fall as many others before them have. Be disciplined to remain in God's Word, for it is your shield and your defense! The psalmist clearly stated, "I have stored up your word in my heart, that I might not sin against you" (Psalm 119:11).

> Let marriage be held in honor among all, and let the marriage bed be undefiled, for God will judge the sexually immoral and adulterous. (Hebrews 13:4)

Avoiding Lack of Discipline and Paying Attention to Detail

Another great vice men are susceptible to is the lack of discipline to fully live out what a man is supposed to be in a marriage. Many men arrive at their home tired and overcome by the stresses of the workday and proceed to immediately disconnect from reality. Men will sit down and watch a television show, go play golf, escape to the quiet repose of an office, or make use of any other type of distraction to find respite from the day's woes–all the while, his wife and family are left unattended to and wanting for attention. This runs counter to the demands of a healthy marriage as proposed by God Himself. Marriage, as understood in the Christian-Judaic sense, entails a man who disciplines himself to become all things for his family, just as Christ is to the Church. A man should purposefully structure his time and appropriately pay due attention to his wife and her needs, to his children and their struggles, to his home and its requirements. Being tired is not an excuse for being a lazy sluggard and failing to lead as a man should.

Our culture today encourages people to fulfill their every desire, regardless of what effect it may have on those around them. This selfishness in the context of a marriage is a recipe for disaster. There is perhaps no greater example of failure than a man who takes his marriage oaths and then proceeds to shirk the responsibilities of raising a family and leading his home. Society as a whole suffers greatly because of cowardly men who selfishly seek their own interests above all else, leaving behind broken families and fatherless children.

It is a proclivity of man to constantly seek more, to want and desire what he does not have. But the Bible warns against this. In Ecclesiastes 4:6, Solomon described the vanity of man's pursuit of riches: "Better is a handful of quietness than two hands full of toil and a striving after wind." Wind is something a man simply cannot grasp or hold. This verse is saying a man should be at peace and content with what he has. Sufficient for the day is the hand you have been dealt; be careful what you ask for, as oftentimes great riches come with great sorrow. Man, in his marriage, must guard against the vanity of earthly materialism while forgetting the treasures he already holds.

God does not instruct or command without purpose; there is a deep truth driving the reason for man to fulfill his obligations in marriage. In a spiritual sense, living your marriage according to a biblical definition glorifies God and is a requirement for an obedient Christian to live in submission to His will; for the believer in Christ, this is sufficient enough a reason. But again, God's commandments are not without purpose. Not only does a biblical marriage exemplify Christ's relationship with mankind, but it serves a broader purpose in its contribution to society at large. Healthy marriages indisputably create healthy persons. Healthy persons grow up to form the fabric of society and in turn raise their own families. So it seems that not only should we live our lives and roles in marriage because it honors the God who created us, but it also serves a practical purpose in the betterment of society.

The responsibility placed upon man in a marriage is great, and far too often it is diminished by a self-seeking culture. It is wise for a man to focus on and nurture what he has in his own family; there is no greater treasure. Man should discipline himself to ensure his wife's needs are met, his children are healthy (mentally and physically), and his family is protected from the stupidity of the secular humanist culture that encourages a foolhardy life. This is the greatest calling a man can answer.

Perhaps it goes without saying, but living in such a way is impossible absent the assistance of God, who Himself defined and created marriage. When a man tends as adamantly to his wife and children as he does to his career and hobbies, his home is a much healthier and happier place. By doing so, he cultivates an environment of spiritual health, strength, and godliness, which without his leadership is sorely lacking. A relationship with a lazy man who pays no attention to his responsibilities in a marriage is an undelivered-upon promise. As a result, a woman will seek spiritual and relational support elsewhere, leaving behind a petulant and immature man. Likewise, children will turn to society for a sense of belonging, and they will find it in all the wrong places. If only men would lead their homes as God intended, America would be a better place for it.

Marriage is yet another battlefield upon which man must prove himself the mighty warrior and valiant knight. He must act with honor and discipline himself so as to uphold the image of Christ, while being keenly aware of his emotional state, keeping it under control, and remaining a lighthouse upon which his family can steady themselves in the storms.

Avoiding Woman's Proclivities

A woman has very powerful and uniquely feminine attributes that God created her to possess. She is fearfully and wonderfully made and, when occupying the role intended for her, contributes nothing short of life itself to her family. Man's need for a good woman cannot be overstated. Women play a crucial role in a marriage and in the development of a child's life, from birth and even before, and thus in the very structure of our nation, among many other things. It is often said that behind every great man is a great woman. This is not only true, but perhaps understated to a great degree. Whether that is a wife who upholds and sustains the efforts of her husband against those who would oppose and deter him, a spouse who manages the affairs of the household and perhaps even her career at the same time, or a mother who spends countless hours nurturing, loving, and pouring herself into her children, husband, household, or all of the above, women have an absolutely essential role to play in marriage and society at large.

On the character of an excellent wife, Proverbs 31:10-11 says, "An excellent wife who can find? She is far more precious than jewels. The heart of her husband trusts in her, and he will have no lack of gain." The chapter goes on to describe a God-respecting woman who manages her household, buys property, handles business transactions, imparts wisdom, and teaches kindness to those who will listen. The image of the woman painted in Proverbs 31 is a Christian-Judaic wife and mother–a powerhouse of industrious ability, trustworthiness, kindness, wisdom, and excellence. She is not above or below particular tasks but takes everything into consideration, preparing her household and family for what may come. She clothes them in the cold, feeds them when hungry, and gives of herself in a way no man can supplant because she employs her innate and gender-specific uniqueness. Woman is most powerful when fully embracing her God-given talents and uniquely feminine attributes while surrendering herself to an all-knowing God who says, "Trust Me."

Avoiding Discontentment

Just as men must confront their demons and discipline their inborn desire to rebel against God's prescribed method of living, so too women must understand themselves as viewed through the lens of eternal truth and take specific and conscious steps to counter that which would destroy them and their effectiveness in a marriage. Perhaps one of the greatest among the natural enemies of woman is the proclivity to cultivate discontentment.

As the culture surrounds the average woman and floods her social media feeds with alluring images of an alleged better life and impossibly unrealistic fantasy relationships, it is incumbent upon the wise woman to rightly divide truth from fiction–to see reality amid the falsehoods. Because the old adage "The grass is never greener on the other side" is true, women must be wary of the enticement of false hopes birthed from the nurturing of discontentment. What begins as a small weed of discontentment is watered until it has overtaken the entire garden and chokes out all the healthy plants growing in that same environment. The negative emotional plant grows until all the gardener can see is the discontentment that covers her garden, and she abandons the entire endeavor in search of new soil. Unfortunately, the soil is not the source of the problem, and the good and healthy plants beneath the negative discontentment are left to die.

Metaphorical, of course, my intent with the gardening story is to convey an example of how a woman must guard against tolerating even a small amount of discontentment within a marriage at the peril of allowing her dissatisfaction to become so large it bursts forth upon the relationship in argument and irreconcilable differences. Who are the abandoned healthy plants? It differs in each individual circumstance, but they would be the children, family, husband, and loved ones who rely greatly upon the valuable and essential contributions a woman brings to the family structure. This may materialize differently for each individual woman, but it is not uncommon today to see wives leaving their families in the middle of their lives, searching for the ideal fantasy relationship or lifestyle.

This is not to say that some discontentment is not justified–far from it. But rather, because women are emotionally prone to allow discontentment to take hold in their lives, it is important that dissatisfaction and negative emotional issues be communicated and dealt with at the earliest opportunity, ideally at their inception. Women should leave no room for the wild growth of unhealthy sentiments and uncontrolled emotions that–although they may spring from seeds of truth in their origin–grow to be deceptively false issues that are more destructive than the original issue itself.

Roles, Not Worth

It is not a difference in value that separates men from women in the biblical sense of order–quite the opposite, actually. The Bible conveys that men and women each represent unique character traits of the Creator Himself and so are created to join with one another to complete a portrayal of God's relationship with us via the institution of marriage. Marriage, as defined in the Christian-Judaic sense, is framed within a set of rules and structure that is unique to the institution of marriage itself. The rules that define a godly marriage are there for our enjoyment and our protection as a society–the rules themselves stemming from an all-knowing Creator who understands more about men and women than we ourselves could ever hope to.

For example, while man is called to be the spiritual leader of the Church and his family, and woman is called to submit to his leadership in that regard, the Bible does not attribute this same structure to, say, a business or government position. A wife's submission unto her husband is a sacrifice made willingly unto God, not her husband or any man. It is a form of worship and surrender to a loving Creator and an acknowledgment that His ways are far above our own.

God is always a God of order and organizational structure. As the Creator of marriage, He specifically defined roles and responsibilities by which, if followed, men and women will succeed greatly in their marriages. This is often a struggle for some women who tend to view the order of marriage as defined by God as a challenge to their individuality. Order is often confused with value or worth, but this could not be further from the truth. Marriage is a sacrifice, for both the man and the woman. God structured marriage to require something of the individual. From the man, God requires his undying devotion and physical toil as he bears the responsibility of leading, providing for, and defending his family. As for the woman, she is called to support her husband in that role and submit to his leadership as unto God Himself. This means she is not to judge or base her actions on those of her husband, but rather, in submission to God's understanding, relinquish her sense of control and trust God.

But what does this mean? It means that just as the man is accountable to God for his actions, so the woman willingly surrenders to God in marriage to the leadership of her husband. Of course, the following goes without saying: this only works when the husband is properly fulfilling his role, and the woman hers. Together they form a marriage. Both the man and the woman are to live God's prescribed roles for marriage, regardless of what their spouse is doing. Human beings have a tendency to judge others and base our actions on the actions or responses of others. God, in His infinite wisdom, placed a structure by which this tit-for-tat behavior is eliminated. God's marriage guidelines require each individual to be guided not by the actions of one another but by the requirements of God. Thus, each is responsible in essence to God for their own individual actions, not the actions of their spouse.

Think of the military structure, for example. Is a soldier worth less as a human being than the captain who leads him into battle? Absolutely not. They are both equally necessary and valuable but have simply been placed into different roles and responsibilities for specific and necessary purposes. Structure and leadership are necessary to navigate the entanglements of battle and enemy threats. So, too, marriage is a union, a partnership, an organizational structure, in which each gender, both male and female, recognizes their individual strengths and plays to them in perfect harmony. It is apparent when this symphony is out of tune, because the husband will decry the wife's lack of respect, and she will pronounce his lack of protection and love; all the while, the children watching will suffer, and the mission of marriage will be incomplete.

God, being the Creator of man and woman, possesses eternal knowledge of the individual. He knows your weaknesses, your strengths, your pitfalls, and your emotional proclivities. He understands exactly what men and women need most. He, then, in perfect knowledge, beautifully orchestrated the institution of marriage and how it is to be conducted to both challenge our individual selfishness and provide guideposts by which to navigate the very weaknesses we each possess.

Marriage Belongs to God, Not the World
The secular culture is one permeated by divorce, confusion, fatherless households, insecurity, and selfishness. In contrast to the Christian-Judaic method that God has intended for healthy marriages, the secular humanist attempts to convince men and women that the exact opposite of what God says is true. Their ultimate goal, absent a Creator upon which to rely, is self-fulfillment at all costs. The woman is encouraged to place nothing above her own desires; likewise, the man is encouraged to turn away from difficulty, in pursuit of both pleasure and avoidance. The consequences of this are plain to see: broken homes create broken people. It is no wonder that an incredible number of marriages end in ruin. Marriage as defined by the secular humanist is entirely about self. In contrast, marriage as defined by God is all about others. It's selfishness versus selflessness.

Because marriage and the family unit are where individuals, at the earliest stages of life, learn how to conduct themselves toward others, the institution of marriage itself becomes a crucial battleground in the culture war. While leftists vie for control of the family unit, they implicitly acknowledge the value the family holds in forming and shaping future citizens. America has traditionally supported the Christian-Judaic values and definition of marriage; hence, strong families raise individuals with a trained connection to self-sacrifice, authority, structure, and true love.

These households espouse the ideals of freedom and individual worth while exemplifying the value of both a man and woman fulfilling their natural roles in marriage, just as roles are necessary for citizens in a free and thriving society.

The Left tries to overcome this powerful source of ideology because when they control the family unit, they will effectively take control of future generations. This is why throughout history we see the concept of core family repeatedly under assault in a variety of ways. From communists taking children to reeducation camps to leftists undermining the authority of parents and seizing children to indoctrinate them with their own secular ideologies, the methods and intent are the same. As Christians, we must be ever vigilant to protect our children and our marriages from the secular humanist culture we face today. Likewise, as Americans, we must intentionally oppose this anti-American and destructive attempt at ruining the definition of marriage and family. It is essential to our survival as a culture, and to preserve the American way of life, that children be afforded their natural right to a healthy family structure as well as the input and example of both a man and woman whenever possible.

Chapter 8

Leadership

What is leadership?

The temporal success of a single incident in and of itself is not proof of an excellent leader. Throughout the multiple public service agencies I've had the privilege of serving with–including the military, several law enforcement agencies, as well as private high-threat security work–I have seen plenty of examples of leadership. Some were good, some were bad; each taught me something about how I should or should not act as a leader.

But, the transcendent example of leadership is found in the person of Jesus Christ, who gave His own life in sacrifice so that others may have life. It is from the Christian-Judaic precepts that we draw the true and greatest examples of servant-leadership. Fortunately for us, the all-knowing Creator of the universe shared His wisdom and eternal perspective in written form so we could always have a guide upon which to rely.

Leadership, as a quality, can be measured by the duality of short-term inspiration of followers combined with long-term results. Essentially, the truthful understanding of leadership is viewed through two lenses: spiritual relevance and practical application (in other words, moral value and common sense). While a short-term victory may yield laudable accolades, the long-term outcome may yet disappoint. I believe it is easy to identify a bad leader; what is truly challenging is learning how to rightly determine whether or not an effective leader is transcendentally good or bad. To frame it simply, there are bad people who are good leaders as much as there are good people who are good leaders, but only wisdom and a firm grounding in reality aid in discerning the difference.

When leadership galvanizes a group, its presence yields immediate inspiration and long-term effects resulting in changed lives. This is only accomplished through servant-leadership–the only true form of good leadership there is.

Ephemeral Leaders

Throughout history, we find many individuals who have exemplified traditional leadership. These examples include a range of people from George Washington and Winston Churchill to Genghis Khan and Mao. Obviously, not all historical leaders are considered good leaders by a moral standard, but they demonstrated leadership traits nonetheless. If there can be bad and good leaders, what is it exactly that defines leadership? You may be temporarily successful in leading a group of followers, but if you ultimately "lead" your followers to their own ruin, are you truly a good leader?

Leaders may be successful, in an administrative sense, in guiding their followers to temporary success while ultimately leading them to a permanent demise; this is the ephemeral leader. Ephemeral leaders are the ideologues throughout history who conjured great followings with charismatic speeches, energetic confrontation of common sufferings, and the ability to convince others of an idea. While those traits, in and of themselves, are not wrong, the deep moral ineptitude and forthright evil demonstrated by many of these leaders, combined with their abandonment or alteration of absolute truth, has been the cause of great human suffering. One cannot help but think of Hitler, Mao, Ahab, Nero, and Jim Jones. All of these are examples of charismatic individuals who used their innate ability to lead blind constituents to certain death, like lambs to the slaughter. Leadership traits? Yes. Good leaders? Absolutely not.

By the secular humanist's standard, many of these individuals possessed leadership traits that were highly coveted prior to the onset of great conflict. Indisputably, some of the known conquerors of the past were capable ephemeral leaders, inspirational to the followers of their time respectively, yet ultimately relegated to the wrong side of history. Therein lies a great truth: the capacity to gain a following in and of itself is not sufficient to define good leadership. One must in good conscience consider the moral, the short-term, and the long-term effects of a leader's actions. In other words, just because you can lead people, that doesn't mean you are leading them to the right place.

Because ephemeral leaders are driven by their finite concept of reality, and often attempt to redefine truth so as to fit whatever narratives they are pursuing, they can become very dangerous–both psychologically and at times even physically. Why? Because those who depart from truth in an attempt to redefine reality find themselves at odds with all persons who do not conform to their will–those who would be an impediment to their end goal. This is why leftists throughout history have committed such horrific atrocities, all in the name of their own "greater good."

Ultimately, these secular attempts at usurping reality have all failed. Yet human pride drives people to repeat what they know to be certain failure. This type of pride in leaders who refuse to abide by truth and live in a realistic state of mind becomes dangerous, because pride of that quantity will stop at nothing to achieve its goals. Ephemeral leaders believe themselves to be lighthouses in the storms of life, but in truth, they are the jagged edges of cliffs upon which all who seek refuge in them find death. Unfortunately, mankind seems determined to repeat the worst aspects of history, so long as it exonerates them from personal accountability. Communists, fascists, and every secular humanist leader in between believed themselves to be original and unique–a demonstrable fallacy. Each new generation embraces their death cult, believing they have discovered the solution to replacing human accountability, but in fact they are no more unique than a single ant in a colony of millions. Excited by the prospect of self-gratification and indulgence, they crucify Christ all over again and attempt to fashion for themselves a golden calf, a replacement of truth that gratifies the immediate and insatiable human desire for pleasure. But each new generation, no matter what form of secular humanism they espouse, meets a similar demise.

These are the leaders one must be on guard against. Without any constant by which to guide their decisions, they are tossed to and fro in the waves of life; those who cling to them always drown.

Abiding Leaders

In contrast to the temporary leadership exemplified in ephemeral leaders of the world, abiding leaders are those whose positive impact goes beyond the temporal because they have at minimum surrendered to the existence of reality and God's Word. They are ultimately in synchronization with a concept or ideology that transcends their understanding or place on the timeline of existence. Unlike the indiscriminate quandary of their secular counterparts, the abiding leader adheres to a constant and immutable ideology upon which they base decisions. These leaders demonstrate a deep connection to eternity; their leadership transcends time itself as it carries forth the banner of truth. Theirs is a bright-colored banner emblazoned with a golden word: wisdom.

The Christian-Judaic worldview relies not on the greatness of man and his elevation but rather on man's depravity and need for salvation. So then, the abiding leader is not defined by their singular or innate ability alone, but rather by their ability to recognize truth and reality outside of themselves. This allows there to be a constant where there is usually confusion and disorder. The abiding leader persists, not in the power of their own might, but rather in the constant reality that is the truth of God, their Creator. The Christian-Judaic worldview derives its precepts not from man's best efforts or psyche, but from the eternal knowledge and guidance of the Creator of the universe and all life. Make no mistake, America's founding fathers knew this and applied it in the creation of the American republic.

This means the Christian-Judaic precepts that direct abiding leaders determine the followers' actions–not the leaders themselves. In this framework of leadership, when the leader fails, the followers can hold him accountable because there exists a higher determiner of truth than the leader himself. The wisdom of God is to the abiding leader what the Constitution is to the American republic: a constant plumb line, not defined by mob rule, which changes with the wind, but by the unchanging aspects of truth set forth in reality itself by the Creator. This is why Americans should be ever vigilant against those seeking to tear down or undermine the key tenets of our Constitution–it is the guide by which we define ourselves as Americans.

This simple truth allows a free, liberty-based governance, not determined by any single individual and even less by a mob but rather by immutable truths defined outside the confines of humanity itself, by the Creator. In the United States, this biblical concept was applied in the form of the Constitution, a unique and essential guiding document. Upon the Constitution, the country is able to base decisions and hold government accountable outside the opinion or leadership of a person, much like the Bible for the Church. No mob, no politician, and no foreign enemy can redefine truths that are self-evident and eternal. Placed into the Constitution, these truths make America a republic, not a democracy.

There are really two sides to this equation: first, the follower who shows the capacity to discern between something right and something wrong; second, the leader who demonstrates the ability to guide the follower toward wise destinations. When these two are brought together, powerful outcomes ensue. The United States of America had always been a shining example of this potent combination, possessing a homogenous Christian-Judaic worldview, which allowed for the above marriage to occur. America was comprised of followers who were united in a common understanding of moral truth and leaders who believed it their humble destiny not to draw glory for themselves but for the transcendent purpose of serving others; this is servant-leadership.

It should be unequivocally stated that it was this marriage of wise followers to wise leaders that in fact allowed America to correct wrongs in such a powerful and effective way. American slavery, being a great evil, was eradicated because of the moral drive of Christians who stood against it and like-minded leaders willing to sacrifice even their own lives for the purpose of truth and righteousness. Similarly, it is the Christian-Judaic remnant that stands alone against the onslaught of socialist cultural warfare today and preserves what remains of the American republic.

Men and women who uphold Christian-Judaic precepts are leaders who exemplify the concept of servant-leadership. Servant-leaders understand their sole purpose is to serve those in their charge and provide them whatever they need to succeed. This includes the idea of giving even one's life as an example for those close behind them and discipling the next generation to do the same. But why would someone give their life for those they are leading? The answer lies squarely in the individual's understanding of eschatology–what happens at the end.

When a united group of individuals believes that life's purpose could be summarized in its eternal value as compared to the fleeting physicality of earthly pursuits, their perspective shifts greatly from that of their secular humanist counterparts. Purpose comes to be defined by the metaphysical, with the ultimate gain being eternal as compared to finite. As clearly understood in context, the Bible presents righteous actions being worth the sacrifice because nothing in this life compares to the truth of eternity that God ordains. We see fear repeatedly countered by the understanding of God's ability and reality within the framework of eternity versus finite moments. Matthew 10:28 says, "Do not fear those who kill the body but cannot kill the soul. Rather fear him who can destroy both soul and body in hell." The idea here is that understanding and living the truth of both moral and physical correctness far outweigh the fragility of any earthly threat or harm that one may face, because ultimately death is not the end. To that point, the apostle Paul said in Philippians 1:21, "For to me to live is Christ, and to die is gain." The servant-leader, emboldened by eternal truth and righteousness, can stand in the face of anything this world has to throw at them; even in death the servant-leader continues to lead. Practically, we see this in the difference between secular humanists, who have no hope beyond this life as they carry their finite and depressing belief into every conflict, and those whose hope is in providence and boldly proclaim, "Death, where is your sting?" (1 Corinthians 15:55).

Servant-leaders exhibit behavior contrary to the secular perspective that life's purpose is the pursuit of self-gratification, the leftist's assumption being that existence is finite and must be lived to the fullest at any expense so as to ensure one has consumed every ounce of pleasure within reach. The worship of self reigns supreme in the secular structure of purpose. It guides their every action, so that no matter how disguised the intentions may be, the ultimate goal is in fact self-serving. This undoubtedly taints the leftist's concept of leadership and their decision-making process when facing the need to sacrifice one's self-gain–be it physical or prestigious, permanent or temporal. When faced with one's sudden demise, the secular humanist has only the preservation of self to consider. Selfish actions always supervene when the godless are caught between exposure and preservation, unless the servant-leader is acting upon something greater than themselves.

As Christ Himself demonstrated, the eternal is far more valuable than the temporal. When heading toward His certain death, fully aware of the suffering that was imminent, Christ prayed to God in the Garden of Gethsemane. Jesus asked if any other way were possible to avoid the horrific death He would face at our expense, yet He willingly surrendered to the metaphysical and eternal will of God with the words "Not as I will, but as you will" (Matthew 26:39). That is servant-leadership. It was not because He believed He would somehow be saved from the excruciating death on a Roman cross. Quite the contrary, actually–Christ knew that the eternal value of His temporal suffering was far greater than avoiding physical suffering at history's most crucial moment. By His selfless actions, everlasting life was ushered into man's reach. He knew it; He believed it; and He led others to the same life eternal. It was Christ's eternal perspective and understanding, His wisdom and fear of God, that makes Him the greatest leader to have ever lived. Christ not only led an exemplary life on earth but continues to lead mankind into eternity and truth still today.

The person of Jesus as the ultimate example of leadership greatly influenced decisions and actions taken by America's early founders. They were among those who wholeheartedly accepted the divine nature of Christ and believed without a doubt that these biblical concepts must be taught to generation after generation of Americans at peril of losing the republic. Because they believed that life was more than the physical reality seen around them, they wove eternal concepts into the very fabric of the newly founded American nation. From the earliest schoolhouses to universities and higher education, biblical instruction was a mandatory component of the thriving American culture. Tragically, secular humanists today have convinced many in our nation that Christian-Judaic values have no place in public education. Not only is this a historically inaccurate belief, it is a single point of failure with grave consequences.

The founders believed that it was the Christian-Judaic worldview that would persevere and maintain the great experiment upon which they had embarked. They believed the Christian-Judaic worldview determined and defined common character traits and crucial institutions such as virtue, marriage, government, and, of course, leadership. Because they accepted one important tenet–life was created by God, and actions taken during that life would ultimately be accountable to Him–society adhered to a higher standard than mankind had ever seen before, and Western civilization flourished. Individuals and smaller groups had abided by these precepts in the past, but America was the first to holistically implement a biblical framework into the constitution of government itself.

If this were not clear enough through the plethora of historical accounts proving so, one may examine the powerful words of John Adams himself, from a letter he wrote to Thomas Jefferson:

> The general Principles, on which the Fathers Atchieved Independence, were the only Principles in which, that beautiful Assembly of young Gentlemen could Unite. . . . And what were these general Principles? I answer, the general Principles of Christianity, in which all those Sects were United. . . . Now I will avow, that I then believed, and now believe, that those general Principles of Christianity, are as eternal and immutable, as the Existence and Attributes of God.[1]

Choose Your Leaders Carefully

Whether you realize it or not, you are following someone or something. Unfortunately for the relativists of the world, there are only ever two outcomes to a decision: you either choose right or choose wrong—life demands absolutes. Just as conceptual law enables us to mathematically calculate physical certainty, so too in realism there is a binary result; no matter what you choose, in the end, it is either right or wrong.

How then can you possibly navigate the complexity and grayness of life? How can the variables that make up the intricacy of even a single day be confined to a binary outcome? I submit to you that man can no more act righteously in and of himself than he can count the stars in all the known and unknown universes. The founders agreed with this very simple concept: the fear of God is the beginning of wisdom. And one cannot be a good leader unless they are wise.

Intelligence yields a finite following, and prowess may fool the naive, but wisdom will lead nations and leave a lasting effect that transcends the life of its possessor. Proverbs 3:13-14 says, "Blessed is the one who finds wisdom, and the one who gets understanding, for the gain from her is better than gain from silver and her profit better than gold." The eternal value of seeing beyond the finiteness of life enables an individual to make deeply informed and valuable decisions. Wisdom therefore becomes the categorically necessary trait of anyone posturing themselves to lead.

On the topic of understanding, instructing, leading, and acting wisely, Solomon made it very clear in Proverbs 1:7, "The fear of the LORD is the beginning of knowledge; fools despise wisdom and instruction." Because the founders believed this and America practiced this, the United States of America was greatly blessed. The caveat? Depart from the belief in absolute truth at your own peril. Should a nation depart from basing their cultural standard on reality and instead pursue the self-pleasing dangers of secular humanism, it will collapse faster than it believes possible. It has happened so often in the past, and we are fools to think we are exempt from the laws of cause and effect. This is why leaders who, at a minimum, are instructed in and understand the application of Christian-Judaic values are essential to the healthy existence of Western civilization. Therefore, leadership as understood by the classical American is defined within the context of the ability to apply and live the precepts of a biblical worldview.

Chapter 9

Motives

What are motives?

Do motives behind actions really matter as long as the outcome is good? The answer is yes . . . and no. Let me explain. As with all aspects of life, the Christian views motives through a bifurcated lens–the lens being the Christian-Judaic worldview through which the individual has both an (a) eternal and (b) finite perspective on life.

The Harmony of the Eternal and Finite Motives

While motives certainly matter in this life, the Christian understands that it is God who works all things according to His will. This is why no matter what occurs in our short and vanity-filled lives, all things work according to what God intended from the beginning. Therefore, while motives may have very real effects, whether negative or positive in this life, ultimately it is the Creator who works all things toward His will. Yet the revealed Word of God informs the Christian that in God's sovereignty, He has created human beings with free will. God's Word shows us that the allowance of man's free will and God's sovereignty work in perfect harmony. Only man's attempt at framing an infinite God in a finite portrait can complicate what is so plainly obvious: God is both sovereign and the giver of free will. In fact, without free will there is no love, and without love one has redefined the character of God. "According to His foreknowledge" is the ever-present thorn in the detractor's side, who would stoop to insinuate that God cannot allow mankind a say in the happenings of their lives, presuming the reduction of His sovereignty–worship of knowledge is the driving force behind this worldview. Yet, despite the degrees and academic achievements, it is the simplicity of the gospel that dispels the wisest of scholars, and the gifting of the Holy Spirit that enlightens the simplest man to a plane above his own capacity.

Motives matter greatly to a Creator who made people in His own image because, given the capacity to choose, man is held accountable by God for his choices; no other circumstance is viably just. Take for example the story of the ten lepers who Jesus healed in Luke 17:11-19. It was the lepers who sought an encounter with Jesus. Of course, He knew they would come, but they initiated their contact nonetheless as they waited for His arrival. Jesus, recognizing the lepers for the incurable diseased individuals they were, extended healing to all of them, not just one or two, but all. Yet, despite all ten leapers being healed, one might say being "offered salvation" from their affliction, only one returned in recognition of Jesus as God and was truly healed both spiritually and physically. Luke told us only the one individual, after he was healed of his affliction, came back in recognition of who Jesus really was. Jesus said in verse 17-19, "Were not ten cleansed? Where are the nine? Was no one found to return and give praise to God except this foreigner? . . . Rise and go your way; your faith has made you well." So, we see Jesus emphasizing two things here: (1) the individual who returned was a "foreigner," a "non-chosen" individual one might say–a clear message against the narrative of only a select few being the chosen ones for salvation, and (2) His salvation was offered to all people–their lack of faith, i.e., lack of response to God's gift of salvation, kept them from spiritual regeneration at that moment. They said no to God. Jesus told the one who returned: "Your faith has made you well." This is a definitive and impactful statement solidifying the doctrine of regeneration being both God-initiated and faith-responsive. That is to say, two things are true at once: God is sovereign, and in His sovereignty, He allows man a choice. This neither reduces God's deity nor elevates man's position, but rather highlights the depth of love that God has toward an undeserving humanity.

Accordingly, the Christian believes that even sorrow and great tragedy can turn out for good by a variety of means over a variety of lengths of time. Motives, therefore, matter in the short run, but in the long run they cannot escape fulfilling an eternal purpose. The free will of man, unquestionably tied to the very character of God and His love, works inseparably with the sovereign authority of God. Therefore, motives are necessary attributes of the obedient Christ-follower, indifferent to what place on the timeline you are considering. Additionally, they matter on a different scale depending on whether or not one is considering individual accountability or the grander scheme. What I mean exactly is, an individual who commits great wrong is to be held personally accountable for their actions, while simultaneously they may be accomplishing an eternal purpose because of God's sovereign nature.

Simply put, you are not excused from the consequences of making bad decisions because you are to live your life obediently to God and you will be held accountable for decisions you make. At the same time, God, knowing man's faults and failures, works all things per His purpose, weaving a timeline of events, good and bad, to accomplish His ultimate plan. Having seen the past, present, and future, He determines outcomes based on His will and man's choices–this is the not-so-difficult mystery to grasp. All of Scripture works in synchronization to show us the glory of the Father through the sacrifice of the Son. Christ's sacrifice then in turn is offered in perfect resolve to all mankind who are willing to respond in faith, so that God remains just. Sovereignty is in no way diminished by a loving God; to the contrary, a finite perspective limits His character to that of a fatalist deity who is incapable of allowing free will. Just because God knows you're going to do something, it does not mean He stops you from doing it. Instead, as the apostle Paul said in Romans 8:28, "We know that for those who love God all things work together for good, for those who are called according to his purpose." Justice and love in perfect harmony–this is the simplicity of truth requiring childlike faith revealed to us in Scripture.

Eternal Motives: The Christian's Life

The eternal perspective is the lens through which the Christian understands that physical life comes to a quick end, life is short, and actions have an impact beyond the immediate. Not all fulfillment is attained while on this earth; therefore, the motivations behind actions may be long in demonstrating their worth. The apostle Paul understood this well when he said, "For me to live is Christ, and to die is gain" (Philippians 1:21). Despite heavy persecution and numerous sufferings, Paul understood that a person's life is nothing in comparison to eternity. Therefore, it is better to serve a greater purpose, namely obedience to God, than be caught up in the finite comforts of compromise. To complete that thought, Jesus said, "What does it profit a man to gain the whole world and forfeit his soul?" (Mark 8:36). Whatever finite rewards one believes they have obtained in the short duration of their life, those rewards pale in comparison to the expanse of eternity and the consequences of rejecting absolute truth–God's truth.

Knowing what steps to take, possessing understanding of both "the now" and "the eternal" in light of God's existence, is called wisdom, the beginning of which is the fear of God. The fear of God is the respect and understanding of His eternal character, His will, and His Godhead. To fear God is to submit to His will in recognition of where one rightly stands in light of eternity and God's true nature. When Jesus spoke with the woman at the well in John 4:23, He said, "The hour is coming, and is now here, when the true worshipers will worship the Father in spirit and truth, for the Father is seeking such people to worship him." I have long pondered Jesus' words when He said, "in spirit and truth," and one cannot help but consider the opposite of those Jesus referred to as being sought by the Father. The antithesis of those the Father seeks are those who acknowledge God's existence but fail to place their trust in His saving grace.

A true Christian is one who has spiritually been made new through the redemptive blood of Jesus and thus worships in the truth, which properly comprehends the purpose of Christ and His relationship to mankind. Jesus directly opposed the religious notions of fulfilling a series of tasks that allegedly grants forgiveness or appeasement of guilt; that is religion. The works-based religious understanding of faith was wholeheartedly rejected by Christ, and while liturgical acts of worship certainly show the inward condition of the heart to a degree, the spiritual manifestation of God's love in one's life is a far greater example of the work of the Holy Spirit. Understanding God's character and His redemptive grace marks the true believer, who exemplifies His love toward mankind outside the confines of the liturgical church structure.

Matthew Henry, in his commentary on this particular assertion of "spirit and truth" made by Jesus, said, "The way of worship which Christ has instituted is rational and intellectual, and refined from those external rites and ceremonies with which the Old-Testament worship was both clouded and clogged. This is called true worship, in opposition to that which was typical."[1]

God takes motives seriously. Clearly, we may be able to deceive those around us for some time–even perhaps for the entirety of our lives–but make no mistake: God is not deceived. Before our feeble lives begin, God has seen every thought and action, and taken into consideration the motives of our heart. This is why surrender to truth is imperative for the Christian–because for the individual wishing to live within the confines of reality while simultaneously pleasing God, there is no other alternative. God's truth is the only truth. Jesus Himself said it best in John 14:6: "I am the way, and the truth, and the life. No one comes to the Father except through me." This assertion Jesus makes is unequivocally exclusive. He does not offer a variety of paths to eternity. He does not consider the way one feels about the reality of existence. Nor does He offer alternative means to those unwilling to abide by truth's standards. No, Jesus, in an incredible demonstration of love, presents an exclusive truth, because truth is exclusive, and this is the only way to truly and realistically love someone.

Upon seeing that there is one absolute truth and one absolute way of obtaining eternal life, the motivations behind every action we take are inextricable from what we as individuals believe; our beliefs often define us, thus absolute truth should define our beliefs. Beliefs are tied to motives, and motives are what define true worship–in spirit and in truth, spiritually redeemed by the only Redeemer and truthfully living a worshipful life in right understanding of our relationship to God. To reiterate, because it's worth repeating, God will not be deceived. You may be able to deceive those around you, even those closest to you, but you will never and have never deceived the all-knowing Creator who spoke light into existence and holds the universe in the palm of His hand. In Galatians 6:7, Paul clarified any remaining confusion on the matter: "Do not be deceived: God is not mocked, for whatever one sows, that will he also reap."

A redeemed individual, having been born again and made anew, will demonstrate the reality of their transformation by truthfully living out the knowledge of God, fostering their relationship with Him, and worshipping Him accordingly. While works are not the path toward salvation, they are certainly the evidence of it. You may be wondering, "What does worshipping *in spirit and in truth* have to do with the notion of motives?" Make no mistake, they are one and the same. A person who rightly understands who they are in light of God's eternity conducts himself in all things so as to bring glory to God; this is worship. Worship is a lifestyle that is born of the knowledge of God and His eternal Godhead. While it often manifests itself in liturgical form, it is no less an act of worship to serve one's fellow man and obey the Word of God in the mundane or minute details of one's life. The motives in one's heart are what make their actions worshipful or not. It is the motives of the heart that separate the sheep from the wolves, the proud deceivers from the humble servants. Motives manifest a person's true beliefs into actions. When motives are knowingly incorrect or wrong, the individual's deception and darker intentions will eventually be revealed, even if that isn't until they stand at the precipice of eternity. The Bible makes this clear in Matthew 7:22-23: "On that day many will say to me, 'Lord, Lord, did we not prophesy in your name, and cast out demons in your name, and do many mighty works in your name?' And then will I declare to them, 'I never knew you; depart from me, you workers of lawlessness.'"

Motives matter.

Eternal Motives: Western Civilization

The Bible emphatically states, "Are we to continue in sin that grace may abound? By no means!" (Romans 6:1-2). Our motives are evidence of a life renewed, and the actions we take demonstrate the condition of our heart. These actions can be spoken, lived, demonstrated, or counseled, but ultimately whether our fellow men see these deeper catalysts or not, God does. Because the Creator sees our internal motives at every turn, we can better understand the depth of which the Christian-Judaic worldview permeated the founders of the American republic. Imagine for a moment how adhering to the understanding of motives and God's eternal truths affected the fledgling American culture as it grew into existence. I submit to you that the founders, and by and large America as a nation, embraced the concept of God's providence and ultimate control in the affairs of mankind and knowingly submitted to a standard of living deemed acceptable to God. When this standard failed, as it inevitably does whenever human beings are involved, it was those same convictions that drew men into bitter conflict to resolve the matters.

Slavery, a great evil in American history, was ended in the

United States through much bitter suffering and pain. In warfare the likes of which the American people have not seen since its time, the American Civil War wrought havoc and violence upon a young nation, with death tolls still prevailing among many other wars combined. It was, without dispute, the Americans' adherence to belief in Christ's eternal truths that drove their convictions to the point of laying down their very lives in the dismantling of moral turpitude. Americans did not die by the hundreds of thousands because of loosely held beliefs. They did not lay down their lives on America's own soil because they believed that God's moral truths should be distinctly separate from government! No, it was their deeply held Christian-Judaic convictions that drove them to commit the selfless acts which shaped the nation because they held as fact that a nation should be founded on none other than the moral principles found in the Bible.

It was this same belief in God's providential intervention that allowed the founders themselves to press forward against astronomically difficult odds. They undoubtedly considered God's truth to be of greater value than their own thoughts or fears. When a nation believes that God's truth is greater than their own thoughts and surrenders to absolute truth instead of being drowned in the quandaries of relativism, then and only then will their efforts thrive. Why? Because efforts premised on false notions or lies about reality cannot, by definition and common sense, lead to anything other than failure. If you believe that you can change your species from human to, say, giraffe, no amount of wishful thinking, plastic surgery, emotional support, or combination of all the above will ever accomplish what you desire. You are not a giraffe. So all efforts to become so will fail because they are premised on a lie.

Why do motives matter in society and in politics? Motives are important because they are the reason behind action. Understanding the reason allows you to predict the future. How so? When you know what someone's intentions are from the beginning, you can tell where they're going. So, intentions and motivation are very important when looking to discern right from wrong and, in the greater scheme, in understanding where a course of action is leading. When we consider politicians or leaders in general, it is important as a member of society and especially as a Christian that you examine their motives and intentions so that you know where their decisions are going to take you.

Unfortunately, we live in a society devoid of attention and wisdom, a society ripe for leftist indoctrination. We have a generation that's only living in "the now," only considering what happens today or this week. They are entirely self-absorbed, saturated by a culture that encourages the worship of self and taking actions based only on the benefits to you as an individual, not society as a whole. When you're only focused on yourself, it's difficult to see where you're going. If you're walking down a hallway and you're staring at your feet, you are never going to see the hard wall until you run into it. Societal movements and cultural shifts are no different. When the focus of a society is completely inner gazing, they are unable or unwilling to pay attention to the motivations of those leading them. The outcome of this could be disastrous. If people are obsessed with themselves and are only staring down at their feet as they walk forward, there is no way they can see what's happening around them or what direction they are heading.

This is how political leaders in a country are able to take advantage of citizens and essentially lead them in whatever direction they desire. Blindly following political movements without consideration for the leaders' motives is a terrible neglect of one's civic responsibility and an abandonment of the Christian's moral obligation. The blind will continue to follow a bad leader regardless of how negative the outcomes are, regardless of how much pain and suffering it will cause in America, regardless of the personal detriment of doing so, because they have never lifted their gaze beyond their feet. However, ignorance is only bliss for a moment. Eventually, one runs straight into that hard wall and feels the unavoidable pain of doing so. Nations have fallen because of blind followers, and nations will fall again. There is absolutely no reason to repeat the sufferings of those before us! Why allow the same leftist ideology that has destroyed so many nations and brought greater human suffering than any other system of government? We must propagate truth and counter the lies of the enemy before it is too late.

Perhaps one of the most dangerous things about inner gazing while being led forward by unknown individuals is that history repeats itself. What do I mean? Learning from history is very different from repeating history's mistakes. Learning from history is observing mistakes in the past and purposing not to repeat them. Repeating history's mistakes is trying the same thing over and over again, despite a mountain of evidence and failures that suggest we shouldn't.

We see this today in leftism across Western civilization, where we have individuals attempting to repeat the same evil atrocities that gave us the most deaths in one century of recorded history and ignoring the reality of those horrible events. The only way people are able to repeat this over and over again is when leaders have convinced a society to look down at their feet and not pay attention to where they're going. They lie about our history; they lie about where we came from; and they most certainly lie about the motivations behind their actions. This is not hard to see! The evidence is there, openly available. All you have to do is pick up a book or research online. History is written for all to observe.

As Christians we bear an added load of responsibility in this arena. The Bible says that we are to study to show ourselves approved: "Do your best to present yourself to God as one approved, a worker who has no need to be ashamed, rightly handling the word of truth" (2 Timothy 2:15). God encourages individuals to make decisions grounded in facts, to understand the times and the world around them, and to make informed decisions about the direction of their culture and society. America used to believe this. We were founded on Christian-Judaic values, and our republic was constructed for a moral and virtuous people. When we abandon morals and virtue, our republic will most certainly fall.

I would remind today's Christians that America has no king. The government is the people, and the people are the government. Therefore, we are to co-rule and decide the direction of our culture and our society. When we've relinquished our rights and civic duties to a few individuals and instead turned our eyes away from the horizon and down toward our feet, we will certainly pay the price. We are at the mercy of those leading us forward, and when those leading us forward have adopted the very ideology of our enemies, we are doomed. We are now at the precipice of great failure.

It all depends on the people to awake, rise, and press forward unto truth. America once believed in natural law, derived from the Creator, who created life with intent and purpose. In large part this was true because of Church leaders who stood for righteousness and were unashamed of the gospel of Christ. It is Satan himself who has convinced the American Church to shirk its civic responsibility in favor of apathy. What a great shame upon our nation that the Church, the very guardian of morality and all that is good, has surrendered to the secular-approved perspective of non-involvement. Not only is this wrong, it is something God will hold every church leader accountable for because as we see in Scripture, silence can be viewed as approval. Such was the case with Esther as we see Mordecai reminding the queen, "For if you keep silent at this time, relief and deliverance will rise for the Jews from another place, but you and your father's house will perish. And who knows whether you have not come to the kingdom for such a time as this?" (Esther 4:14).

Chapter 10

Sacrifice

What does it mean to sacrifice, and why would anyone do such a thing?

Parents lose sleep to care for their children. People work untenable hours to feed and care for those they love. Soldiers offer their very lives on the battlefield. What do they all do it for?

Sacrifice can only be understood when viewed through the lens of one's worldview, which is what a person holds to be true and most valuable about the world. No one willingly dies for something they don't believe. As culture drifts away from absolute truth, and beliefs are increasingly self-centered rather than premised on the social standard of Western civilization, where does that leave our future? Who will sacrifice for freedom and peace if there are none who believe in causes worthy of sacrifice? If good has been rejected as a reality in favor of relativism, who then will charge forth to conquer evil–both figuratively and literally?

I submit to you that sacrifice, and therefore great feats of righteousness, is incumbent upon one's understanding of reality and eternal purpose. You will not suffer for something if there is nothing you believe in worth suffering for, much less will you die for it. In this chapter, we will explore how sacrifice is understood in Western civilization and what happens when absolute truth is abandoned in favor of the self-worshipping cult of secular humanism. Let us clarify and examine the topic of sacrifice and what it means to the American republic, the Christian, and those who have sacrificed much throughout history.

Finite Pain Is Worth the Eternal Outcome

To understand sacrifice, we must first consider its meaning within the context of what it costs the individual to do something–namely, what level of pain is endured in relation to the action taken and its intended outcome. This inevitably places an individual's understanding of sacrifice on a scale with varying degrees of application. It may cost me relatively little to wake up earlier in the morning than I desire and go to work; on a pain scale this is a sacrifice most individuals count as worthy in relation to the benefits of receiving a steady paycheck. But consider for a moment the extreme level of that pain spectrum, like for those who spoke out against the Nazis in Germany. Theirs was a very real and severe pain. Theirs was a pain worth enduring as per their understanding of life being firmly planted in worthiness of their cause: the resistance to Hitler's atrocities and the belief that good indeed conquers evil in the end.

An eternal perspective on right and wrong drove countless individuals in the twentieth century to sacrifice greatly, including giving their very lives. This was a perspective grounded in the firm belief that secular humanism is evil as compared to the Christian-Judaic worldview. It is the Christian's understanding of the eternal that drives them to complete virtually any effort, even to the point of death, so long as it is aligned with God's perspective, His Word, and His plan to save mankind. Western civilization's foundational understanding of sacrifice is this: good is worth dying for if it is in furtherance of defeating evil and standing for truth.

We see this level of pain that is worthy of enduring demonstrated in the person of Jesus. In Philippians 2:8, the apostle Paul wrote of Jesus: "Being found in appearance as a man, he humbled himself by becoming obedient to death–even death on a cross!"

(NIV). So, it begs the question, what did Jesus believe was worthy of dying for? For Christ it was God's eternal purpose and intention to save mankind by offering Himself as the propitiation for all sin–undoubtedly a worthy cause for which to suffer pain, and Jesus did so willingly. As Christians, we are called to live as ambassadors of God, as living representations of Christ and His purpose. This, according to the Bible, is best accomplished by how well the Christian endures suffering and pain. As Paul clarified in Romans 5:3-5, "Not only that, but we rejoice in our sufferings, knowing that suffering produces endurance, and endurance produces character, and character produces hope, and hope does not put us to shame, because God's love has been poured into our hearts through the Holy Spirit who has been given to us."

It would do the Church today good to consider how they may suffer for Christ's sake.

Sacrifice is worth it because truth is worth infinitely more than a lie. The courageous individual will never again turn from truth once it's been discovered, because having seen reality, it is impossible to deny it. Paul exemplified this as an individual who had everything by worldly standards–status, acumen, power–yet he counted all of it as rubbish when he discovered the value of the knowledge of Christ. Paul wrote in Philippians 3:7-8, "But whatever gain I had, I counted as loss for the sake of Christ. Indeed, I count everything as loss because of the surpassing worth of knowing Christ Jesus my Lord. For his sake I have suffered the loss of all things and count them as rubbish, in order that I may gain Christ." Paul made clear in this letter that possessing the knowledge of Christ and believing God are the definition of faith, and thus the premise for everlasting life. Thus, it follows that if the possession of the knowledge *of* Christ, combined with the subsequent placement of faith *in* Christ, leads to everlasting life, there is no earthly measure by which to quantify the value of Christ and what He offers the individual; on this foundation one can suffer, knowing that pain is but for a moment and life is eternal.

For the Christian, this pain is viewed as finite, temporary, even fleeting, as life lasts only for a short time and then eternity calls. Matthew 16:24-26 makes the Christian's perspective on suffering and pain very clear: "Then Jesus told his disciples, 'If anyone would come after me, let him deny himself and take up his cross and follow me. For whoever would save his life will lose it, but whoever loses his life for my sake will find it. For what will it profit a man if he gains the whole world and forfeits his soul? Or what shall a man give in return for his soul?'"

For the Christian, everything in life is about Christ and obedience to Him; there is no other cause worth sacrificing for. His eternal redemption makes sacrifice, even unto death, absolutely worth the cost.

Often the anti-theist will point to the undeniable existence of evil in the world as reason for their denial of a higher power. Others will claim no overarching goodness can exist while evil is so prevalent in the world. The Christian-Judaic perspective takes the exact opposite stance and submits that the very existence of evil is definitive proof of the existence of good. How can something be defined as evil if not identified by a standard of good? If there is a defined evil, then what or who defined good by which evil is measured? If there is a moral law, there is a moral lawgiver. When adopting the perspective of the secular humanist, evil becomes all that exists in the finite mental perspective, and thus actions, purpose, and ultimately the causation of sacrifice become muddled between emotions and survival of the self. Thus, for the secular humanist, what they are willing to sacrifice for, both individually and on a grander scale, becomes something completely different from the homogenous understanding of sacrifice in Western civilization. As the world moves into a godless state of governmental worship, the reasons behind people's actions at all levels of society are drastically altered, inevitably leading to very different outcomes when compared to previous Christian-Judaic concepts in society.

Sacrifice, by definition, is costly. People's willingness to suffer for a cause greater than themselves is directly correlated to the great historical outcomes in our fledgling history as Americans. In other words, what people believed determined what they were willing to sacrifice. As the history of Western civilization has proven, this eternal mindset produces those who view life through an eternal lens, self-sacrificing individuals who count it worthy to suffer for the sake of others, as Christ Himself exemplified. This homogenous cultural belief in eternal purpose and causation led Americans specifically, though not uniquely, to accomplish great feats in the name of freedom, but it didn't start there. Throughout all of human history we observe individuals who aligned themselves with God's purpose and willingly suffered so others might live.

Pain and Suffering in Sacrifice
Pain is a most difficult concept for people to grasp. Those who understand pain and are not dismayed from enduring it in service to others are the individuals who comprehend the true value of pain, and thus comprehend sacrifice accordingly. Pain, when understood, becomes less of a foe than one might first believe, and understanding pain increases the ability to accomplish great tasks.

Understanding pain is the catalyst of greater sacrifice. It is the Christian-Judaic perspective on God's sovereignty and eternal purpose that molds the Christian's worldview regarding pain and suffering. The Christian never denies the existence of evil; they acknowledge it as a physical and metaphysical reality and understand it within the confines of God's saving grace. This is why the Christian does not kill for God; they die for Him–die to self, die to others, die so as to make way for a greater truth, die so that others may live. Of course, this does not always mean a literal death, though that has been a reality for many Christians throughout history. What the Christian means by "dying to self" is a moving aside of the prioritization of self so that there no longer exists any impediment to observing God's truth. Therefore, through suffering, the Christian illustrates the eternal value of God's truth to others. Suddenly, for the one living in spirit and in truth, the finite pain of this world is fleeting, and eternity casts a cloak of tolerability on the suffering individual. All at once there is hope in the midst of despair. This is what Christ does for the accepting individual–those who willingly submit to God's will and grace.

Many individuals decide whether or not to take a certain action based solely on what it will cost them–in other words, what they must sacrifice to make it so. So it follows that the individual's understanding or belief concerning pain and suffering in light of their worth and vanity becomes quintessential to their actions. Our actions as Christians pivot on our understanding of eternity. Let me be clear about this point: for the Christian, there is no action worth taking if the preceding forethought is not steeped in deeper theological comprehension of the eternal. What do I mean? Sacrifice is absolutely worth the pain if eternal purpose is the ultimate result–that is to say, if there is a greater purpose than this life, if there is a cause worthy of giving one's life for.

Life, as a race upon which we embark, is fraught with pain, suffering, disappointment, and heartache, yet the Christian endures for the sake of Christ's truth. We achieve the impossible along the way; as the apostle Paul clarified in Philippians 4:13, "I can do all things through him who strengthens me." Because of truth we waver not on our journey. We run, as Hebrews 12:1 says, "with endurance the race that is set before us." As with any great cause, sacrifice is worth the price contingent on the outcome. In the Christian's case, the outcome is eternal life and God's glory–a life of leading others to the knowledge of the God who loves them. In light of tremendous persecution and physical suffering, Paul clarified the importance of this eternal reality: "If in Christ we have hope in this life only, we are of all people most to be pitied" (1 Corinthians 15:19). In no uncertain terms Paul stated that if what we believe is not true, we are wasting our time and are fools for doing so. Paul continued to dismiss the abysmal reality of death, which every soul in due time must taste, and reenforced the hope that belongs only to those in Christ. Paul, the highly educated and respected former Christian-killer turned Christ-follower, said in

1 Corinthians 15:58, "Therefore, my beloved brothers, be steadfast, immovable, always abounding in the work of the Lord, knowing that in the Lord your labor is not in vain." Sacrifice, when seen in eternity's light, becomes an acceptable venture, which Christ provides the strength to endure.

Belief in Action

Throughout all of human history, Christians have sacrificed greatly for the purpose of God's glory and bringing others to the saving knowledge of His truth in Jesus the Messiah. I do not allude only to the Christian martyrs who, in laying down their lives so that others may live, paid the ultimate price for believing in Jesus (though they certainly are deserving of laud), but also to the warriors such as the American founders and many others throughout world history who stood their ground for truth, who embarked upon cataclysmic journeys trusting that God's hand was sustaining them. Let us consider those who have gone before us and the sacrifices they made.

In the first century, there lived a man named Polycarp. Polycarp was a very young man when first appointed bishop of the church in Smyrna. He served for many years there as the pastor and teacher of the believers in what is today western Turkey. Polycarp studied under the apostle John, who, of course, knew Jesus personally. It is believed that Polycarp wrote several letters to first-century Christians, but one is most notable: his letter to the Philippian church. Polycarp was hunted by Romans for his refusal to offer sacrifices to the Roman emperor during the Fourth Persecution under Emperor Marcus Aurelius Antoninus and was eventually found and arrested. According to the English historian and martyrologist John Foxe, in his work *Foxe's Book of Martyrs*, Polycarp was exhorted by the Roman proconsul to deny Christ and be saved: "Swear and I will release thee! Reproach Christ," he said. But Polycarp refused. At eighty-six years old, Polycarp, the pastor of the church of Smyrna, was burned alive for refusing to deny the truth of Jesus Christ. Foxe recorded his words: "Eighty and six years have I served [Jesus], and he never once wronged me; how then shall I blaspheme my King, who hath saved me?"[1]

Polycarp was not nailed or tied to the stake as was usual because he assured his captors he would stand firm and not run away. Polycarp did not immediately die because the wind blew the flames away from his body and the fire danced around him in an arc. Upon realizing this, a Roman soldier stepped forward and pierced him with his sword. It is said that so much blood poured forth that it extinguished the flames. Polycarp died a martyr with his faith intact. One might objectively observe that so sure was Polycarp's faith in Christ, he was willing to die a horrific death in refusal to deny the truth of God. This undoubtedly exemplified to anyone under his leadership, and perhaps many others, the value and worth of Christ's saving grace. He never denied Jesus but demonstrated a powerful example of truth and his conviction of reality, so much so that he was willing to die so that others might know the truth as well. That is sacrifice–truth is worth dying for.

During the same era of persecution, there was another man named Germanicus who, Foxe stated, was "a young man, but a true Christian, being delivered to the wild beasts on account of his faith, [who] behaved with such astonishing courage that several pagans became converts to a faith which inspired such fortitude."[2] As was the case with many Christians before and after him, Germanicus was fed alive to wild animals because of his faith in Christ. Such was his belief that as he exemplified the Christian strength found only in God, several of those who watched him valiantly die became themselves converts to Christianity. Germanicus's behavior during his suffering led others to an eternal existence well beyond the fleeting ailments of this finite life. That is sacrifice.

Why would men like Polycarp and Germanicus go to their deaths instead of denying the reality of Jesus? What did they see that would cause them to hold such strong convictions? I believe they saw the same thing that everyone sees more than once in their lifetime: the yearning and unequivocal calling of one's Creator, which when answered leads to a complete transformation of one's soul: a new creation is born, from which there is no coming back or denying.

The Christian-Judaic worldview not only emboldens and inspires great acts of self-sacrifice but also the everyday labors and struggles of the person attempting to live a godly life and bring others to the same. In the 1600s, Samuel Rutherford preached throughout Scotland and suffered varying types of persecution, albeit not physical. He was banned from preaching due to his stance on weak theology. Rutherford would in his lifetime lose his wife and two of his children, yet he was never dismayed from pursuing what he believed to be the ultimate goal in life: teaching others about God's truth. Rutherford himself wrote in 1631, "The great Master Gardener, the Father of our Lord Jesus Christ, in a wonderful providence, with his own hand, planted me here . . . and here I will abide till the great Master of the vineyard think fit to transplant me."[3] Rutherford's adherence to a biblical worldview and his understanding of God's purpose in his life sustained him through various trials and allowed him to sacrifice on behalf of others, to persevere where others would fail, for the sake of absolute truth, namely the truth of Christ.

Faith Versus Human Secularism in American Culture

Christians throughout the ages have shown proof of the truth they carry with them, by their exemplary actions and incredible acts of sacrifice amid trials, which have indisputably had a profound and lasting effect as evidenced by Western civilization. Consider for a moment the national effect of Christian-Judaic beliefs on the newly born American colonies as well as the subsequent reality that everywhere Western philosophy has spread, the world has become more free, more equitable, and more successful economically than ever before in history.

We know that the biblical worldview was highly influential in all early institutions of the United States because of meticulous writings and records that we can view for ourselves today. Even those who were not explicitly Christian by definition agreed with the notion of upholding Christian-Judaic values in society because it appeared to them, in contrast to failed ideologies of the world at that time, to be the best way to achieve freedom and liberty. It was Christians who stood against and ultimately defeated the practice of slavery in the Western world. It was Christians who demanded fair and equal representation of individuals by their government. It was Christians who drove charity and concern for the less fortunate for much of the existence of the United States. It was Christians who ensured that those of other faiths or no faith at all still maintained the same equal rights as those of Christians, and who fought to keep government out of private life as much as possible. The revision of secular humanism would like you to believe that the freedoms and liberties uniquely catalyzed by the United States would be entirely possible without the foundations that made it so; this is emphatically a lie. Without Christian-Judaic values in America, there would be no Western civilization as we know it today.

It is more than apparent that the American founders based virtually every institution on biblical precepts. From the words of George Washington to Benjamin Franklin, our history is replete with biblical references and implications. The Bible is the most quoted source by the American founders, and their actions in recorded history tremendously reinforce their biblical values. One could write endlessly on the divine intervention the founders saw during the American Revolution, and they did not shy away from stating as much. This belief is inextricable from the precepts taught in the Word of God, poignantly including the concept of sacrifice, which the founders were well familiarized with. Death was their close friend, but God their best.

Take, for example, the state of affairs during the presidency of John Adams, the second president of the United States. The French Revolution was at hand, and the United States was threatened by the possibility of war yet again. Adams had written to former president George Washington and requested he return to serve his country once again as the commander of the Continental Army in expectancy of a war with the French. Let us take a look at their own writings, their own words and sentiments, in the context of our focus on sacrifice, and let us examine their perspective of the subject in light of impending doom.

Washington himself believed it was God who prevailed during the Revolution and was clear and articulate about his belief. He believed in exhausting every peaceful means possible and would not enter into conflict until righteously compelled to do so. He echoed his wartime sentiment in his response to President Adams, as he emphasized his belief that it was God who led them to victory during the Revolution, and that God's purpose was evident in their pursuit of liberty. In response to President Adams asking him to return and take command of the American army once again, he wrote this on July 13, 1798:

> Satisfied therefore, that you have sincerely wished and endeavored to avert war, and exhausted to the last drop, the cup of reconciliation, we can with pure hearts appeal to Heaven for the justice of our cause, and may confidently trust the final result to that kind Providence who has heretofore, and so often, signally favoured the People of these United States.[4]

It is beyond obvious that Washington's faith emboldened him to conduct great acts of sacrifice on behalf of others–in this case, his nation–because he believed that God's truth was to be primary in man's list of earthly pursuits. So great was the cause of liberty that Washington, understanding life to be finite and but a whisper of the eternal glory to come, thought it worth even dying for to advance the cause of truth and defend the nation he believed God Himself had established. Washington's words "trust the final result" reinforce his biblical perspective that it is God who determines man's outcomes, not man himself, and that sacrifice to this end is worth the pain one would endure for a righteous cause. This undoubtedly is derived from Washington's knowledge of Scripture, where Christ Himself taught us that God's will is cause for sacrifice, even to the point of crucifixion. In the Garden of Gethsemane, Jesus "fell on his face and prayed, saying, 'My Father, if it be possible, let this cup pass from me; nevertheless, not as I will, but as you will'" (Matthew 26:39).

Or perhaps it was Washington's familiarity with the story of Abraham, who when called upon by God to sacrifice his only son Isaac did not question or doubt but pressed forward toward that end knowing that God was always in the right, and ultimately seeing that God's plan was for Abraham to trust Him and rest in His sovereign provision. The American founders would have learned, as Abraham learned, that faith in God is counted as righteousness, believing that God is who He says He is, and that placing one's trust in Him–not one's own strength or efforts–ultimately leads to salvation.

President Adams himself echoed these sentiments when he, in official capacity as president of the United States, declared a National Day of Prayer and Fasting over the impending war with France. President Adams wrote in 1799,

> The most precious interests of the people of the United States are still held in jeopardy, by the hostile designs and insidious acts of a foreign nation, as well as by the dissemination among them of those principles subversive of the foundations of all religious, moral and social obligations, that have produced incalculable mischief and misery in other countries.[5]

William Federer noted in his book *America's God and Country: Encyclopedia of Quotations,* that Adams was referencing the American universities at the time that had meddled in the French concepts of infidelity or lack of faithfulness. Adams continued:

I do hereby recommend accordingly, that Thursday, the 25th day of April next, be observed, throughout the United States of America, as a day of solemn humiliation, fasting and prayer–That the citizens, on that day, abstaining as far as may be from their secular occupations, devote the time to the sacred duties of religion, in public and in private: That they call to mind our numerous offences against the Most High GOD, confess them before him with the sincerest penitence, implore his pardoning mercy, through the Great Mediator and Redeemer [Jesus], for our past transgressions, and that, through the grace of his Holy Spirit, we may be disposed and enabled to yield a more suitable obedience to his righteous requisitions in time to come.[6]

It is undeniable, regardless of the mountain of revisionism we face today, that the founders minced no words in pronouncing their belief in the God of the Bible and the saving grace and message of Jesus Christ. This is a factual statement, and inarguably so. Hence it goes without saying that the founders' understanding of sacrifice was derived from the very same biblical precepts upon which they based virtually all other public, private, and governmental declarations and actions, including the most severe of all actions to be taken by standing governmental representatives: that of declaring or preparing for war.

John Adams was, without a doubt, familiar with and educated in biblical doctrine. He understood its application to society both publicly and privately. Adams was surely familiar with the account of Jehoshaphat's prayer in 2 Chronicles, a situation much like the one he found himself in as president in 1799. Jehoshaphat, then ruler of Judah, had only recently brought about great reform in his kingdom, and his success was entirely due to his willingness to purge the land of pagan practices, like worshipping false gods such as Baal, and practicing child sacrifice. Jehoshaphat turned the people away from this evil and back to their founding in the one true God. Moreover he revamped the governmental structure, appointing judges and rulers over spiritual areas, government areas, and local magistrates. Of course, no turning to truth comes without a spiritual challenge, and shortly after, news arrived of the Moabites, Ammonites, and Meunites who had gathered together to destroy Jehoshaphat and the nation of Judah. They took particular issue with Judah's holiness and rejection of regional gods and practices. The situation was dire! It was the godless world versus the one true God and His chosen people; this was a time for Judah to experience the true meaning of sacrifice. The kingdom of Judah would either bend to the will of those who opposed God and His commandments or stand for truth and face a much larger, more powerful force seeking their destruction.

Upon hearing of the mighty nations who had assembled to destroy Judah, Jehoshaphat declared a national fast. This was a time for everyone to appeal to God for salvation and guidance. Ultimately, Jehoshaphat trusted in God's victory and chose to obey and remain faithful, even going so far as to place musicians in front of the soldiers as they marched into battle. The musicians were instructed to sing and worship God as they entered the field of warfare. In 2 Chronicles 20:12, Jehoshaphat clarified his worldview by saying to the Lord, "We are powerless against this great horde that is coming against us. We do not know what to do, but our eyes are on you."

God prevailed, and Judah's enemies were destroyed as they turned against one another in battle prior to Judah's army even arriving at the engagement. God proved Himself faithful to Jehoshaphat regardless of circumstantial obstacles, just as He said He would.

Thus says the LORD to you, "Do not be afraid and do not be dismayed at this great horde, for the battle is not yours but God's. Tomorrow go down against them. Behold, they will come up by the ascent of Ziz. You will find them at the end of the valley, east of the wilderness of Jeruel. You will not need to fight in this battle. Stand firm, hold your position, and see the salvation of the LORD on your behalf." (2 Chronicles 20:15-17)

Judah's enemies were destroyed, and it was not by their might or prowess but because of their acknowledgment of an eternal perspective, that of a saving God who commands even the enemies upon a battlefield. Their submission, eternal perspective, and obedience to God's will allowed them to sacrifice when it mattered the most.

John Adams, at the helm of the fledgling nation faced with the possibility of international conflict once again, feared the United States would not endure another great conflict at that time. Adams, much like Jehoshaphat, appealed to heaven in a desperate hour, when faced with an impending war. After declaring a National Day of Prayer and Fasting, Adams went on to complete his presidency without having gone to war. His diplomatic efforts, driven by his Christian-Judaic convictions to seek peace at all costs, in the end paid off. In 1800, just after he had finished his term, the French agreed to peace.

Much like Jehoshaphat, our founders cast their fears upon God. They believed that an adherence to God's way of doing life, of doing government, of doing civil society, was the only way to be set apart from the rest of human history and man's attempt to craft for himself a success story apart from God's influence.

As noted above, in the year 1800 France signed a peace treaty with the United States. But in contrast to the subsequent super growth in the United States, France went on to suffer tremendously in their pursuit of secular humanism and embarked on a crusade to rid their nation of any trace of Christian-Judaic influence. As is historically the case with virtually all secular humanist efforts to deify the state, it resulted in widespread violence and death. In contrast to what was occurring in the United States, the French Revolution ignited violence and death across their country.

Theirs was a secular humanist campaign to destroy the Christian society and all its influence. Churches were burned; pastors and priests were executed on the spot; hundreds of thousands died in the secular purge that sought to remove all influence and trace of Christ from French society. It's estimated that 600,000 to 1.3 million French died during the war periods. Some 17,000 were executed during what is now recognized as the Reign of Terror, and another 10,000 French died in prison without ever having a trial.

In contrast, the United States during this same period experienced tremendous growth and Christian revival. There were men like Charles G. Finney, who believed the gospel was not only to save man's soul but useful as a means of cleaning up society. Finney was himself a strong abolitionist and believed Christians had an obligation to be involved in antislavery efforts. According to Dr. Diane Severance, in a 2010 article titled "The Second Great Awakening,"

> Christians became the leaders in many other social concerns such as education, prison reform, temperance, Sabbath observance, and women's rights. The large numbers of Christian workers for social reform became so influential, they and the organizations they founded became known as the Benevolent Empire. The Second Great Awakening had a greater effect on society than any other revival in America.[7]

This was the result of a nation turning back to God in every conceivable way–not hiding, not cowering, but allowing God to be the God of every aspect of life, both public and private. It was this mindset that allowed early Americans to suffer and sacrifice greatly for causes they believed worthy of dying for–causes such as fighting for freedom, defeating slavery, expanding education, teaching biblical doctrine, defending the defenseless, and freeing others to do the same.

In concluding the discussion of sacrifice and what it means to the Christian, and in a broader sense to the American, it is conclusive that Western civilization's perception of sacrifice is entirely dependent on one's acceptance of the biblical perspective. It was Winston Churchill who perhaps summarized it best in concluding that Western civilization was inextricable from Christian-Judaic values. It was amid the greatest struggle of Britain's existence that Churchill said, "I expect that the Battle of Britain is about to begin. Upon this battle depends the survival of Christian civilization."[8] Churchill understood that if the secular humanist mentality of the Nazis were to prevail, the world would enter a globally dark period the likes of which had never been seen before. Fortunately there was a group of nations who still upheld the Christian-Judaic values of individual worth and liberty, whose sons and daughters were sent by the millions to sacrifice themselves on the altar of freedom and peace; they understood the value of sacrifice. They laid their lives down, knowing that we live for but a moment, and thereby ensured the peace and freedom of millions in generations to come.

Let us never forget their efforts, nor those of the countless brave who have gone before us–those who submitted first to the reality of a loving Creator who designed them with purpose and gave them the ability to accomplish great tasks for the sake of others. We must not lose touch with the biblical notion of sacrifice and its influence on Western civilization, or else the next time we face a global darkness, the outcome may be quite different.

> Do not neglect to do good and to share what you have, for such sacrifices are pleasing to God (Hebrews 13:16)

Endnotes

Chapter 1: Truth

1. G. K. Chesterton, *What's Wrong with the World* (Manchester, NH: Sophia Institute Press, 2021).
2. Rob Stroud, "C. S. Lewis and Self-Awareness," Mere Inkling Press, February 19, 2020, https://mereinkling.net/2020/02/19/c-s-lewis-and-self-awareness/.
3. Alexander H. Stephens, "Cornerstone Speech," March 21, 1861, https://www.ucl.ac.uk/USHistory/Building/docs/Cornerstone.htm.
4. "Democratic Opinions on Slavery! 1776-1863," Library of Congress, https://tile.loc.gov/storage-services/service/rbc/rbaapc/07610/07610.pdf.

Chapter 3: Purpose

1. Friedrich Nietzsche, *The Gay Science* (1882, 1887), para. 125; ed. Walter Kaufmann (New York: Vintage, 1974), 181-82.
2. Nietzsche.
3. Richard Weikart, *From Darwin to Hitler: Evolutionary Ethics, Eugenics, and Racism in Germany* (London: Palgrave MacMillan, 2006).
4. Jason Lisle, *Fractals: The Secret Code of Creation* (Green Forest, AR: Master Books, 2021).
5. "The Mandelbrot Set," Complex Analysis, https://complex-analysis.com/content/mandelbrot_set.html.
6. Lisle.
7. John Adams, "From John Adams to Massachusetts Militia, 11 October 1798," Founders Online, https://founders.archives.gov/documents/Adams/99-02-02-3102.

Chapter 4: Pride

1. Saul D. Alinsky, *Rules for Radicals* (New York: Vintage, 1989).
2. Aleister Crowley, *The Equinox of the Gods* (London: BM/JPKH, 1936).
3. William J. Federer, *America's God and Country: Encyclopedia of Quotations* (Saint Louis, MO: Amerisearch, 2000).
4. Walter Isaacson, *Benjamin Franklin: An American Life.* (New York: Simon & Schuster, 2003).
5. Federer.
6. Federer.

Chapter 5: Self-Defense
1. R. J. Rummel, *Death by Government* (Piscataway, NJ: Transaction Publishers, 1994).
2. "Article 2, Section 1, Clause 7," Records of the Federal Convention, https://press-pubs.uchicago.edu/founders/documents/a2_1_7s2.html.
3. Jacques Mallet du Pan, *Considerations on the Nature of the French Revolution and on the Causes Which Prolong Its Duration* (London: 1793).
4. William Federer, *America's God and Country: Encyclopedia of Quotations* (Saint Louis, MO: Amerisearch, 2000).
5. Federer.
6. Aleksandr Solzhenitsyn, *The Gulag Archipelago* (New York: Harper & Row, 1973).
7. Susan Ratcliffe, ed., *Oxford Essential Quotations*, 5th ed., "Mao Zedong 1893-1976," https://www.oxfordreference.com/display/10.1093/acref/9780191843730.001.0001/q-oro-ed5-00007069.

Chapter 6: Gender
1. Mary Kay Linge and John Levine, "Over $200K Being Spent on Drag Queen Shows at NYC Schools, Records Show," *New York Post*, June 11, 2022, https://nypost.com/2022/06/11/over-200k-being-spent-on-drag-queen-shows-at-nyc-schools/.
2. Pamela Newkirk, "Diversity Has Become a Booming Business. So Where Are the Results?" *Time*, October 10, 2019, https://time.com/5696943/diversity-business/.
3. Alexander Hall, "Bud Light's Marketing VP Was Inspired to Update 'Fratty,' 'Out of Touch' Branding," New York Post, April 10, 2023, https://nypost.com/2023/04/10/bud-lights-marketing-vp-was-inspired-to-update-fratty-out-of-touch-branding/.
4. William Haupt III, "Op-Ed: The Naked Communist, 60 Years Later," Center Square, February 17, 2020, https://www.thecentersquare.com/national/op-ed-the-naked-communist-60-years-later/article_dad8f2bc-51aa-11ea-bb87-6336083758e9.html.
5. Haupt.
6. Susan Ratcliffe, ed., *Oxford Essential Quotations*, 5th ed., "Mao Zedong 1893-1976," https://www.oxfordreference.com/display/10.1093/acref/9780191843730.001.0001/q-oro-ed5-00007069.

7. Robert J. Morgan, *100 Bible Verses That Made America* (Nashville, TN: Thomas Nelson, 2021); George Washington's Circular to the States, June 8, 1783, https://www.mountvernon.org/library/digitalhistory /quotes/article/i-now-make-it-my-earnest-prayer-that-god-would -have-you-and-the-state-over-which-you-preside-in-his-holy -protection-that-he-would-incline-the-hearts-of-the-citizens-to -cultivate-a-spirit-of-subordination-and-obedience-to-government -to-entertain-a-brotherl/.

Chapter 8: Leadership

1. "John Adams to Thomas Jefferson, 28 June 1813," Founders Online, https://founders.archives.gov/documents/Jefferson/03-06-02-0208.

Chapter 9: Motives

1. "Matthew Henry Commentary of the Whole Bible," Bible Study Tools, https://www.biblestudytools.com/commentaries/matthew-henry -complete/john/4.html.

Chapter 10: Sacrifice

1. John Foxe, *Foxe's Book of Martyrs* (1563).
2. Foxe.
3. "Samuel Rutherford Quotes About Jesus Christ," AZ Quotes, https:// www.azquotes.com/author/12820-Samuel_Rutherford/tag/jesus -christ.
4. "From George Washington to John Adams, 13 July 1798," Founders Online, https://founders.archives.gov /documents/Washington/06-02-02-0314.
5. "Fast Day Proclamation, 6 March 1799: https://founders.archives.gov/ documents/Adams/99-02-02-3372.
6. "Fast Day Proclamation, 6 March 1799."
7. Diane Severance, "The Second Great Awakening: Its Story and Impact," Christianity.com, June 23, 2023, https://www.christianity .com/church/the-2nd-great-awakening-11630336.html.
8. Winston Churchill, "Their Finest Hour," International Churchill Society, June 18, 1940, https://winstonchurchill.org/resources /speeches/1940-the-finest-hour/their-finest-hour/.

About the Author

Josiah O'Neil grew up in South America as the son of Christian missionaries who preached the gospel of Jesus to those they felt called to serve. His parents instilled in their five children a deep appreciation for the Christian-Judaic principles America was founded on.

At the age of seventeen, Josiah joined the United States Army and served as a combat medic during combat operations in the Sunni Triangle regions of Iraq. After honorably discharging from the army, Josiah went on to conduct private military contract work, again deploying to the Iraqi region, mainly conducting High Threat Protective Operations for the U.S. Department of State.

After his overseas service, Josiah joined the Los Angeles County Sheriff's Department and served for several years before transferring to a local police department in Southern California to serve as a patrol officer. Josiah later returned to the Foreign Service but this time as a Special Agent with the United States Diplomatic Security Service, a security and tactical arm of the U.S. Department of State.

Due to the unforeseen death of his father, Josiah, his wife, Lindsay, and their three children–Scarlett, Emma, and Connor–returned to California, and he served as a Deputy Sheriff in the County of San Diego, where he had the privilege of working a variety of roles.

In 2022 Josiah ran for U.S. Congress in California's 49th Congressional District. While not advancing to the general election, Josiah understood the importance of working to uphold our values and institutions, now more than ever. Josiah left government service after almost twenty years to operate his own private security consulting group and that same year founded Defining Truth, a non-profit aimed at articulating America's worldview, reintegrating Christian-Judaic values into civics, and encouraging the Church in America to reclaim roles they once held in public spheres of influence.

After being a public servant for most of his life, Josiah felt the unequivocal call to take a stand in America's culture war. As we see the erosion of our society's morals and values daily, and the deceptive revision of our nation's true origins, Josiah believes that now is the time to stand and define truth. He has resolved not only to talk about the issues that plague our nation, but to actively create real and lasting change. Josiah believes the people of America deserve to be represented by their government and should have access to non-revised historical facts concerning the origins of our great and exceptional country. But, more importantly, there is a need for Americans to acknowledge the providence which sustained them and blessed them excessively and realize the loss to come should they turn from God in all aspects of civic and personal life.

Stay Tuned for Josiah's next book "Why It Matters!" coming Fall 2024

Amidst the confusing world of politics, many have forgotten why our values matter to the American way of life. "Why it Matters" explores specific topics in depth and provides an apologetic defense to reason with and defend Christian-Judaic values in politics.

For more information check out Defining Truth's website by scanning the QR code here, or going to www.definingtruth.org

SCAN HERE

Lindsay and Josiah O'Neil

Josiah O'Neil and Derek Baray
Circa 2021 Sheriff's Department

Recommended Books

If you are interested in further equipping yourself to engage the culture, I recommend the following books, amongst many others of course, as they have been influential in my understanding of civics and defending American values.

- *Politics According to The Bible* Wayne Grudem
- *50 People Every Christian Should Know* Warren Wiersbe
- *The Treacherous World of The 16th Century* William Federer
- *Who Is The King In America* William Federer
- *Well Versed: Biblical Answers to Today's Tough Issues* James Garlow
- *Unshakeable Foundations: Contemporary Answers to Crucial Questions About the Christian Faith* Norman Geisler and Peter Bocchino
- *Ultimate Proof of Creation: Resolving the Origins Debate* Dr. Jason Lisle
- *Letter to The American Church* Eric Metaxas

· INTEGRITY ·
FAMILY · DILIGENCE
EST. 2022

DEFINING
TRUTH NO COMPROMISE
JOSIAH ONEIL

Defining Truth (DT) is a non-profit organization founded by Josiah O'Neil with the purpose of equipping and engaging the culture with a Christian apologetic worldview. Does marriage between a man and a woman matter today? Is abortion really a necessary hill to die on? The answer to both is yes, but why should it matter to a non-Christian? Defining Truth tackles these questions and many others, providing the *why* behind conservative values in America, and more importantly why we must preserve them at all costs.

DT is developing courses accessible online to teach individuals how to defend specific issues in the culture war, and how to communicate their value to the nation. Additionally, DT produces content online via social media, and actively engages in civic discourse wherever possible. The aim of these various content producing venues is to convince the mass of conservatives, many of whom are church-attending Christians, that civics to the Christian in a Constitutional Republic is the Areopagus to Paul in the first century church. The Areopagus, according to the Oxford Encyclopedia of Ancient Greece and Rome (2021), "was the most prestigious and politically powerful institutions in Athens." According to the book of Acts Chapter 16, Paul was "greatly distressed" by the idolatry and pagan worship, so he engaged the politicians directly with the truth of God as he "reasoned" with them and their philosophy.

We must make every effort to exhort, reason with, and represent God's truth in a dark and dying world.

Josiah, along with co-host Brandon Jones, runs a podcast which airs once a week self-titled "Defining Truth Podcast" in which they discuss headline issues of the week, and how to appropriately interpret these events through a biblical perspective.

Josiah and his wife Lindsay O'Neil also host a second podcast titled "Marriage: A Sacred Union" where they discuss common issues within a modern marriage, and how turning to Christ is the only solution amongst a failing world of divorce and problematic relationships.

As a non-profit, DT raises all operational expenses from like-minded individuals who believe in the mission of keeping America trusting in God, and His guidance. If you would like to support this mission, please consider a tax-deductible donation, or monthly contribution to Defining Truth. All proceeds go to further engaging America in the culture war, and equipping others to carry God's truth into the world around them.

For more information, check out www.definingtruth.org and join the fight!